DISCIPLESHIP
FOR ALL
BELIEVERS

DISCIPLESHIP FOR ALL BELIEVERS

Christian Ethics
and the Kingdom of God

PHILIP LE MASTER

HERALD PRESS
Scottdale, Pennsylvania
Waterloo, Ontario

Library of Congress Cataloging-in-Publication Data
LeMasters, Philip, 1964-
 Discipleship for all believers : Christian ethics and the kingdom
of God / Philip LeMasters.
  p. cm.
 Includes bibliographical references.
 ISBN 0-8361-3579-2 (alk. paper)
 1. Christian ethics. 2. Eschatology. 3. Church. 4. Christian
life—1960- I. Title.
BJ1251.L39 1992   91-36402
241—dc20   CIP

DISCIPLESHIP FOR ALL BELIEVERS
Copyright © 1992 by Herald Press, Scottdale, Pa. 15683
 Published simultaneously in Canada by Herald Press,
 Waterloo, Ont. N2L 6H7. All rights reserved.
Library of Congress Catalog Number: 91-36402
International Standard Book Number: 0-8361-3579-2
Printed in the United States of America
Book and cover design by Paula M. Johnson

99 98 97 96 95 94 93 92 10 9 8 7 6 5 4 3 2 1

*To those who were my fellow students
in the Graduate Program in Religion,
Duke University,
from 1987 through 1990*

Contents

Foreword by Donald B. Kraybill 9
Preface 13

1. Jesus' Resurrection As the Beginning of a New Age 17
    Introduction • 17
    Recent Views of Eschatology and Ethics • 20
    On Apocalyptic • 27
    Theological Construction • 31
    Church As Foretaste of the New Age • 39
    A Distinctive Approach • 43

2. Church As Proleptic Social Locus of the New Age 51
    Toward the Social Production of the Church • 51
    Guidance for the Church at Corinth • 66

3. Moral Description and Practical Reason
    in Eschatological Context 79
    Theological Grounds for a Narrative Description • 80
    Practical Rationality • 85
    Justice • 89

4. Is Discipleship "Sectarian"? 103
    Troeltsch's Church-Sect Distinction • 104
    Gustafson's Temptation • 114
    Medical Ethics • 126

5. Conclusion: Discipleship for All Believers 135

Notes 143
Bibliography 157
Author Index 161
Scripture Index 163
Subject Index 165
The Author 171

Foreword

Controversy over the meaning of the kingdom of God has swirled down through the corridors of church history over the centuries. How did Jesus understand the timing of the kingdom of God? Where can faithful disciples find guidance for righteous living? In the Scriptures, of course, but biblical scholars differ widely on the meaning of even key passages such as the Sermon on the Mount.

Some New Testament theologians argue that Jesus goofed on the timing of the kingdom: its fulfillment which Jesus predicted in his lifetime didn't materialize. According to these interpreters, this theological embarrassment undercuts the authority and integrity of Jesus' teachings, since his entire ethical system hinged on the assumption that the kingdom was about to break in and end the temporal world. If the world was about to end, it made sense to turn cheeks in the face of violence, give away cloaks to beggars, and sell property to benefit the poor. But Jesus, according to these interpreters, was mistaken about the arrival of the kingdom. If he had correctly read the divine calendar, perhaps he would have crafted different ethical precepts— relevant, sensible, practical ones for a world that would be around for centuries to come. According to this prevalent school of interpretation, Christians have to look elsewhere, beyond the teachings of Jesus, for practical and relevant ethical guidance.

The relevance of Jesus' teachings for Christian ethics is also diluted by other interpreters who focus primarily on the future. Stressing the sacrificial, atoning death of Jesus rather than his life or resurrection, these theologians view the kingdom of God as pie in the sky by and by. The kingdom and its perfectionist ethics will bloom in a future age, they say, in another dispensation of grace. Ironically, both of these schools of interpretation, liberal and conservative, render the ethical authority of Jesus meaningless and thus divorce the Bible from social ethics. A Christian social ethic, according to both of these diverse schools of interpretation, must seek a philosophical anchor outside the New Testament.

Moreover, other interpreters insist that those who seek to appropriate Jesus' teachings seriously will end up in the pits of social irrelevance, withdrawn from social discourse with the larger society. Such ethical purists often form sectarian enclaves that shrink from moral responsibility in the social mainstream. These streams of ethical thought leave contemporary disciples of Jesus with three unpleasant options: disregard Jesus' teachings because of his temporal miscalculations, hope for pie in the sky by and by, or withdraw into sectarian cloisters of irrelevance.

In this volume, Philip LeMasters leads us through the moral morass with a rather simple yet radical proposition. He offers a new way of conceptualizing ethics in the kingdom of God. Rather than reconstructing apocalyptic categories, he proposes that ethics in the kingdom of God ought to pivot on the confessed belief in Jesus' resurrection. In brief, the resurrection of Jesus on that first Easter morning has inaugurated a new age in God's kingdom which awaits its final consummation in the eschaton. The disciple of Jesus lives in the tension of the temporal space between Pentecost and Parousia.

By making the resurrection the pivotal starting point, LeMasters lifts us above the old theological debates. We take the teachings of Jesus seriously because they are the words of our risen Lord, but we hear them from an Easter morning perspective. Starting with the resurrection faces us forward, toward the future consummation of the kingdom.

By anchoring our reflection on kingdom ethics on the resurrection, LeMasters provides a new paradigm for understanding discipleship in the modern world. But he does much more. His brief summary of the various positions of Christian ethicists permits us to grasp the essence of the various schools of ethical reflection, to pinpoint their flaws, and to trace the uniqueness of a resurrection-based ethic.

LeMasters aids us in bridging many gaps. With Easter as our starting point, we are able to envision Christian ethics flowing from biblical teaching, not divorced from them. The teachings of Jesus link into the future consummation by way of the resurrection. The historical Jesus and the Lord of history, Pentecost, and Parousia, intersect together in the empty grave.

Although LeMasters contends that the church should function as a community of discernment and a foretaste of the new age to come, such discernment does not lead the church down a sectarian alley. Just the opposite. LeMasters shows how practical discipleship in the shadow of the resurrection leads not to irrelevance but to significant discourse with the major moral issues of our times. Such ethical reflection is not confined to a few elite Christians cloistered in a monastery. Serious discipleship, exuding the joy of the resurrection, is the vocation of all believers.

—*Donald B. Kraybill, Director*
Young Center for the Study of
Anabaptist and Pietist Groups
Elizabethtown College
Elizabethtown, Pennsylvania

Preface

I wish to express my gratitude to a number of people whose efforts have made this book possible. The final product has benefited from criticism of earlier drafts of the entire manuscript by Professors Stanley Hauerwas, Kenneth Surin, Geoffrey Wainwright, and Frederick Herzog. Professor Harmon Smith and Mr. Philip Kenneson graciously gave of their time to suggest helpful revisions of the first chapter. I am grateful for the assistance of these individuals, all of whom are associated with the Graduate Program in Religion at Duke University.

Apart from the influence and support of my parents, Joy and Claude LeMasters, I cannot imagine that I would have developed either the spiritual or intellectual inclination to be interested in Christian ethics, much less to write a book on the subject. Likewise, Paige Humes LeMasters, my wife, has encouraged and sustained me in unparalleled ways throughout the trials and tribulations of writing and revising this document. Words cannot express my profound sense of thankfulness for these three people. God has blessed me through them immeasurably.

I also appreciate the confidence of Herald Press in my work and the editorial efforts of S. David Garber. Though many people have played a role in getting this book into its final form, full responsibility for its limitations and flaws rests with me.

I have dedicated the volume to those who were my fellow students in the Graduate Program in Religion at Duke University from 1987 through 1990 because they are the ones who did the most to hold me accountable to rigorous standards of theological analysis on an almost daily basis during the research, writing, and revision of this book. They helped me wrestle through the issues which are central to the volume. They also saw me through periods of great personal and intellectual discouragement. For their companionship, stimulating conversation, and encouragement, I will always be in their debt.

—Philip LeMasters

DISCIPLESHIP
FOR ALL
BELIEVERS

Jesus' Resurrection As the Beginning of a New Age

Introduction

Ever since Jesus proclaimed that "the year of the Lord's favor" had begun with his ministry (Luke 4:16-21), believers have pondered questions of the nature and presence of God's kingdom in human history. Such questions have often been framed with reference to the sort of life appropriate to those who seek to follow the Lord of the kingdom in discipleship. What does it mean, Christians have asked throughout the ages, to live in faithful response to the demands of God's reign? What does it mean to follow Jesus in the ministry of the kingdom?

This volume stands within that long line of inquiry on the relevance of God's kingdom for the Christian life. Specifically, it establishes a temporal view of the theological and moral significance of Jesus' resurrection as the beginning of a new age which radically contextualizes and shapes the Christian life. It pursues this goal, in large part, by presenting a view of the church as the anticipatory social embodiment of God's fulfilled reign.[1]

In this approach, Christian ethics becomes the communally and temporally located task of following the Lord who will end history by consummating God's kingdom.[2] Between Pentecost (Acts 2) and Parousia (the second coming of Christ, as in 1 Cor. 15:23-28), the locus of discipleship becomes the church. This is the fellowship that imperfectly reflects the subjection to God that will characterize all reality in the *eschaton* (the last thing, the end, as in 1 Pet. 1:5). An implication of the argument is that Christian ethics may not be understood rightly apart from such churchly and eschatological location.

The five chapters of the volume bring together prominent themes of Christian theological and ethical analysis. The purpose is to bring insight on the relevance for the Christian life of the new age of God's kingdom begun in Jesus' resurrection. One important theme of the discussion is eschatology: the relevance for Christian ethics of hope for the coming fulfillment of the kingdom. Another focus of the study is ecclesiology: the nature and function of the church within an eschatological context.

These points of emphasis obviously have a long history of analysis in Christian theology. Our goal is to determine how the interrelation of eschatology and ecclesiology shapes a view of Christian ethics. This ethic is contextualized by an identification of the church as a foretaste of the new age which has already begun in Jesus' resurrection. In other words, the volume seeks to show that eschatology has an important shaping influence for the Christian life in many respects.

The terms *eschatology* and *Christian ethics* obviously have broad reference and have been interpreted in many different ways throughout the history of Christianity. It may, therefore, be helpful to the reader for me to indicate briefly the particular path which our discussion will take. This first chapter establishes the basic systematic point on which the rest of the volume is conceptually dependent: Jesus' resurrection has begun a new age of God's kingdom, created a future, which contextualizes and shapes the Christian life as an endeavor taking place between Pentecost and Parousia. It is precisely this between-the-times location which warrants a view of the church as a foretaste of the fulfilled reign of God through the power of the Spirit (cf. 1 Cor. 10:11).

In this account, the church is empowered by the presence of

the risen Lord through the Spirit to foreshadow the future salvation guaranteed by Jesus' resurrection. Moreover, as the second chapter displays, the church has the profound moral relevance, and the obviously difficult job, of producing and sustaining disciples. These followers are to discern what faithfulness to the risen Lord entails in given circumstances and to manifest in their common life a foretaste of God's reign. In this sense, the Christian life requires an ecclesial context for its intelligibility and sustenance.

This notion of a socially sustained discernment requires careful explication in order to display with precision how it functions and is distinctive from other views of moral rationality. Hence, the third chapter deals with the material relevance of an eschatological, communal view of the Christian life for practical reason and moral description. A dominant view of Christian ethics has suggested that such a mode of moral analysis is "sectarian" in the sense of being entirely withdrawn from social realms other than the church. Therefore, the fourth chapter examines critically the arguments for that view, and suggests that they rest largely on problematic nontemporal eschatological assumptions.

By challenging the adequacy of those arguments, the discussion demonstrates that our approach to ethics may properly be applied to matters throughout a world which is destined for final subjection to God on the basis of Jesus' resurrection. The fifth chapter briefly summarizes the conclusions and immediate implications of the overall argument.

This volume processes a number of distinct conceptual problems and scholarly discourses, including New Testament scholarship, systematic theology, social science, moral philosophy, and theological ethics. Yet the central organizing principle, which holds these divergent concerns together, is precisely the temporal view of eschatology. It enables us to see the resurrection of Jesus as the beginning of a new age of God's kingdom, which one day will consummate in God's final victory over all sin and death. The acceptance of this eschatology leads logically to certain ecclesiological and moral commitments.

Hence, rather than simply a collection of five essays on various theological and moral issues, the book advances one central point: a proper view of eschatology leads naturally to determinate views of the Christian life and the social location and moral analysis that are appropriate to it. Therein is the coherence of the project.

Recent Views of Eschatology and Ethics

In the past century, many theologians and biblical scholars have advanced divergent and influential views on the importance of eschatology for thinking about Christian ethics. As is well known, the tendency of Protestant liberalism was toward an ethical view of the kingdom in easy continuity with the progress of Western culture. For example, Albrecht Ritschl thought of God's reign as a progressively developing moral society,

> the association of [hu]mankind—an association both extensively and intensively the most comprehensive possible—through the reciprocal moral action of its members, action which transcends all merely natural and particular considerations.[3]

That moral view of the kingdom, so important for liberal reform movements such as the Social Gospel, was first challenged in 1892 by Johannes Weiss in *Jesus' Proclamation of the Kingdom of God*. In contrast to Ritschl, Weiss in this book understands Jesus to have preached an apocalyptic kingdom, "a radically superworldly entity which stands in diametric opposition to this world." The kingdom is "never an ethical ideal, but is nothing other than the highest Good, a Good which God grants on certain conditions."[4]

Since Weiss thinks that Jesus wrongly expected the imminent coming of the kingdom, he calls theologians "to mitigate the ardent eschatological tone" of the Lord's preaching.[5] That line of interpretation culminates in the claim that the universally valid element of Jesus' preaching is "not his idea of the Kingdom of God, but that of the religious and ethical fellowship of the children of God." Weiss allows that Christians may speak of this fellowship as the kingdom, but "the admission must be demanded that we use it [*kingdom*] in a different sense from Jesus . . . [for] we do not share the eschatological attitude."[6]

Hence, Weiss's theological appropriation of the kingdom ironically has much in common with the earlier non-eschatological views of God's reign as

> the invisible community established by Jesus and comprised of men [and women] who call upon God as Father and honor him as King . . . and [where] we earnestly endeavor to obtain the highest ethical ideal, that of perfectly fulfilling God's will.[7]

Albert Schweitzer continues the attack on ethical views of the kingdom in his 1901 publication of *The Mystery of the Kingdom of God* and his 1906 book, *The Quest for the Historical Jesus*. Schweitzer locates Jesus firmly in the tradition of Jewish apocalyptic, noting that he proclaimed the imminent coming of God's reign. For Schweitzer, "the Baptist, Jesus, and Paul are simply the culminating manifestations of Jewish apocalyptic thought."[8]

He describes Jesus' message as a "thoroughgoing eschatology" in which the kingdom is entirely future. This teaching called for repentance in expectation of the kingdom's coming, the famous notion of an "interim ethics" applicable only for the short time before the coming of God's reign. Schweitzer claims that, when the kingdom did not come during the disciples' preaching mission, Jesus tried to force the hand of God for its manifestation by his own death. These hopes went unfulfilled, and the kingdom expected by Jesus did not come.[9]

In his *Civilization and Ethics*, Schweitzer comments that Jesus' view of the world is "pessimist through and through as far as the future of the natural world is concerned."[10] Modernity had to overlook that aspect of his teaching, however, to ensure "progress in the spiritual life of Europe."[11] Indeed, Schweitzer's ethics of "reverence for life" is not explicitly or materially informed by Christian doctrine or by his view of Jesus' preaching. He declares, "Ethics originates in my thinking out completely, and trying to actualize, the world-affirmation which is innate in my will-to-live."[12]

Schweitzer's conclusions about Jesus' unfulfilled eschatological hopes leave no room for the present direct relevance of Jesus' teachings and kingdom expectation for the Christian life.

Once Jesus' preaching of the kingdom is rejected, some other basis for ethics has to be found.

Weiss and Schweitzer's positions both insist that Jesus' preaching focused on and was shaped by his expectation of the imminent coming of God's eschatological reign. Their views caused quite a stir among both liberal and orthodox Christians. The liberals were offended by the idea that Jesus' preaching was intended only for his contemporaries during a short time of apocalyptic expectation, not as a timeless truth relevant for modern individuals and social structures. Orthodox Christians, Catholic and Protestant, could not reconcile Jesus' mistaken predictions with his divinity. From the perspective of both scholars, Jesus' kingdom expectation concerned a period long ago and was simply wrong.[13]

C. H. Dodd attempted to put a more congenial face on Jesus' ministry with his project of "realized eschatology." In his writings he suggests that in Jesus' ministry, God's kingdom and the fulfillment of its blessings were already present.[14] He thinks that the kingdom remained present since Jesus' time, and that the Lord's teachings are intended for all Christians, not only for the first generation. While Dodd does not attempt directly to challenge Weiss and Schweitzer, he does seek to display how Synoptic texts that refer to the kingdom as present can be read as a key for interpreting references to the kingdom as future.

Dodd argues for realized eschatology in his 1935 Shaffer Lectures, later published as *The Parables of the Kingdom*. From Jesus casting out demons in Matthew 12:28 and Luke 11:20, he gathers the meaning that "the sovereign power of God has come into effective operation." He reads Mark 1:14-15 and Luke 10:9-11 in light of those passages and concludes that Jesus thought the kingdom to be "a matter of present experience" rather than "something to come in the near future."[15] In *The Apostolic Preaching and Its Developments*, Dodd suggests that elements of futuristic eschatology in the Gospels are the work of later church formulation; the earliest tradition of Jesus' preaching is precisely that of realized eschatology.[16]

Hiers comments that

> Dodd achieved the goal of his apologetic: to refute the idea that
> Jesus had mistakenly expected or proclaimed the imminence of
> the kingdom of God or any other eschatological events. Dodd's Je-
> sus need be no stranger and enigma to modern religious
> sensibility. . . . Jesus could remain the great teacher and guide for
> the moral life of modern Christians.[17]

Dodd's interest in Christian ethics is evident in his *Gospel and
Law: The Relation of Faith and Ethics in Early Christianity.* He
lets Jesus' timeless "ethical precepts" function as "guideposts on
the way we must travel in seeking the true ends of our being under the Kingdom of God."[18] His view of the kingdom as present
provides a way of explaining how both "Gospel and commandment" are relevant to life in the here and now apart from a
scheme of futuristic expectation.[19]

Rudolf Bultmann responds to the eschatological challenge
differently. In *Jesus Christ and Mythology*, he agrees that

> Weiss showed that [in Jesus' preaching] the kingdom of God is
> not immanent in the world and does not grow as part of the
> world's history, but is rather eschatological, i.e., the kingdom of
> God transcends the historical order. . . . God will suddenly put an
> end to the world and to its history, and He will bring in a new
> world, the world of eternal blessedness.[20]

Bultmann rejects Dodd's realized eschatology as unjustified "escape reasoning," as "Jesus clearly expected the irruption of
God's Reign as a miraculous, world-transforming event" in the
near future.[21]

Like Dodd, however, he is greatly concerned to display how
Jesus' preaching of the kingdom is relevant to life in the contemporary world. Toward that end, Bultmann sets out to "demythologize" Jesus' eschatological preaching in order to display
the timeless understanding of existence present in it. According
to Bultmann,

> The one concern in his teaching was that man [and woman]
> should conceive his [or her] immediate concrete situation as the

decision to which he [or she] is constrained, and should decide in this moment for God and surrender his [or her] natural will. Just this is what we found to be the final significance of the eschatological message, that [the hu]man now stands under the necessity of decision, that his [or her] "Now" is always . . . the last hour, in which his [or her] decision against the world and for God is demanded, in which every claim of his [or her] own is to be silenced.[22]

Bultmann teaches that Jesus first came to see human existence as a series of crises calling for decision between the world and God, and that Jesus then expressed that understanding "in the garments of a passing cosmology."[23] The kingdom did not interest Jesus "as a describable state of existence, but rather as the transcendent event, which signifies for [the hu]man the ultimate Either-Or, which constrains him [or her] to decision."[24]

Hiers comments that for Bultmann

Jesus used the categories of apocalyptic Judaism only incidentally; his real understanding, prior to and independent of these categories, can readily be extracted and made central to our understanding. Such a Jesus is no stranger and enigma to modern, at any rate, early twentieth-century existentialist thought after all.[25]

In this way, Bultmann intends to rescue Jesus from the irrelevance for modernity that his misguided eschatological expectations seemed to entail.

Similarly, Bultmann seeks to establish an existentialist basis for Christian ethics in the claim that Jesus' demand for radical obedience is "absolute," relevant for Christians today, and "by no means influenced in their formulation by the thought that the end of the world is near at hand."[26] As obedience requires "the surrender of one's own will for the good of the other [hu]man," Bultmann has difficulty with the Gospels' descriptions of Jesus promising rewards even "to those who are obedient without thought of reward."[27] He resolves that problem by deciding that

the motive of reward is only a primitive expression for the idea that in what a [hu]man does, his [or her] own real being is at stake—that self which . . . he [or she] is to become. To achieve that self is the legitimate motive of . . . ethical dealing and of . . . true obedience."[28]

In this way, self-actualization of the individual as understood in Heideggerian terms becomes the form of Christian ethics.

Bultmann interprets the kingdom's relevance in terms of its claims upon the will in the moment of decision. In his words,

> Jesus knows only one attitude toward God—obedience. Since he sees [hu]man[s] standing at the point of decision, the essential part of [the hu]man is for him the will, the free act. . . . For on will, on free act, depends [the hu]man's existence as a unit, as a whole. . . . The whole [hu]man is evil if his [or her] will is evil.[29]

He argues that the meaning of Jesus' preaching of the kingdom is the call for existential obedience to God through free decision in the present.

Throughout his existentialist moral project, Bultmann locates the meaning of Jesus' establishment of the kingdom in ahistorical, nontemporal categories. He disagrees with Dodd by affirming that Jesus did preach a futuristic kingdom. Yet he demythologizes that expectation to find its relevance purely in the decisions of individual Christians who should treat every hour as "the last hour." Bultmann takes this theological tack because he wants to affirm Christian faith and the relevance of Jesus' teaching while allowing that "it is impossible . . . to believe in the New Testament world of demons and spirits" and live in the modern world.[30]

Implicit in Bultmann's claim is the assumption that an eschatological worldview oriented toward the future of a coming reign of God cannot be the worldview of moderns. Bultmann makes this assertion because his theological project focuses primarily on the relationship of the modern individual to God. He interprets the present significance of Jesus' preaching and the rest of New Testament proclamation in accord with the nontemporal view of the self which his existentialist philosophy assumes.[31]

Bultmann employs the method of demythologizing to recover

the timeless truth of Jesus' preaching of the kingdom in a way congenial to contemporary sensibilities. His method entails the abandonment of the kingdom's relevance for a historical, cosmological salvation. Instead, he favors the kingdom's static relevance for the will of particular individuals. In this way, aspects of New Testament proclamation that point toward a future kingdom of God have no direct shaping influence on the production of Christian theology and ethics. Heideggerian philosophical categories are applied to antiquated scriptural claims in order to elucidate the meaning of the latter.

Amos Wilder makes a similar hermeneutical move in *Eschatology and Ethics in the Teaching of Jesus*. He claims that "not the nearness of the end but the supreme significance of his errand and the resistance from the old order governs the world-renouncing claims" of Jesus' preaching of the kingdom.[32] Jesus uses apocalyptic "fictions" to communicate the importance and urgency of righteousness before God.[33] He "casts his vision of moral consequences into concrete pictures of compensation. . . . The eschatological conception itself . . . rises from the same dramatizing necessity."[34] Jesus calls for repentance and righteousness in "the present time of salvation" through eschatological language.[35] Instead of an interim ethics, Jesus has an "ethics of the time of salvation or new-covenant ethics." The eschatological preaching simply provides a formal means of expression: it did not materially shape its content.[36]

Wilder thinks that the crux of Jesus' ministry is his "summoning of all to a total response of obedience to the Father . . . [and] to a new kind of righteousness."[37] Jesus' preaching

> grew out of the concrete crisis of his situation rather than out of the interpretation of it in apocalyptic terms. The apocalyptic event in the future is essentially of the character of myth.[38]

Wilder's similarity to Bultmann lies in his view of apocalyptic as a husk within which lies the kernel or real meaning of Jesus' preaching. Though without Bultmann's explicit existentialism, he comments that Jesus demands that we have an

immediate relation of obedience and response [to God]. The full
personal will of the individual is therefore in play. This is a point
that Bultmann makes much of. Ethics is now unqualifiedly the relation of the heart to God, person to Person, and this is ever present and controlling in the relation of [hu]man to [hu]man.[39]

Wilder is critical of Bultmann at points. Yet he shares with
Bultmann the view that the meaning of Jesus' eschatological
preaching is to be found in individual decision apart from the direct relevance of temporal expectation for a coming kingdom.
In this way, eschatology does not materially inform, shape, or
control ethics: it simply provides a form for its expression.[40]

Thus Weiss, Schweitzer, Bultmann, and Wilder accept a view
of Jesus as an apocalyptic figure who wrongly preached the imminent coming of God's reign. They think that Jesus' teaching
must be subjected to a thorough reinterpretation in order for it
to have relevance for life in a world that has not and will not become God's perfect kingdom. Within this context, Weiss returns
to a liberal ethical view of the kingdom, and Schweitzer aban-
dons the task of *theological* ethics altogether. In contrast, Bultmann and Wilder continue to interpret the kingdom in static existentialist terms. Dodd responds in another way to this eschatological challenge. In order to sustain the present religious and
moral relevance of God's reign, he rejects the claim that Jesus
maintained a futuristic view of the kingdom.

On Apocalyptic

Norman Perrin's doctoral dissertation, *The Kingdom of God in
the Teaching of Jesus*, documents and evaluates much of this
century's biblical scholarship on Jesus as an apocalyptic figure.
Perrin concludes that the debate has

> established that the Kingdom is both present and future in the
> teaching of Jesus. The discussion has reached this point; Weiss
> and Schweitzer were not able to convince the world of scholar-
> ship that it was wholly future. Dodd was not able to maintain his
> original [realized] view . . . , and Bultmann's wholly futuristic in-
> terpretation was modified [by his students].[41]

Given this conclusion, Perrin continues the debate with his own view of Jewish apocalyptic's impact on Jesus' preaching of the kingdom. He notes that apocalyptic expectation was characterized by "an immensely elaborate conception of the end of this present age and the beginning of a new and wholly different one." Various construals of apocalyptic were "so manifold . . . that it is impossible to reduce them to a systematic picture . . . [as] variety and plasticity belong to its very nature."[42]

Yet "this bewildering complex of expectation" contains two central themes for Perrin: "God's decisive intervention in history and human experience, and the final state of the redeemed to which the intervention leads."[43] From an analysis of several Gospel texts, he concludes that Jesus' view of the kingdom is apocalyptic in "precisely these same ways" of the emphasis on God's intervention and the final state of the redeemed.[44]

Perrin's comments demonstrate how reserved the conclusions of the historical-critical study of Jewish apocalyptic have been. On his reading, apocalyptic concerns a diverse genre that is characterized by a scheme of future expectation for some type of divine intervention that relates in some way to the final state of the redeemed. Jesus' preaching fits somewhere within that vague matrix of expectation.

Recent scholarly attention to apocalyptic has produced similarly formal descriptions of the genre. For example, the Society of Biblical Literature Genre Project defines apocalyptic as

> a genre of revelatory literature with a narrative framework, in which a revelation is mediated by an otherworldly being to a human recipient, disclosing a transcendent reality which is both temporal, insofar as it envisages eschatological salvation, and spatial, insofar as it involves another, supernatural world.[45]

John Collins in *The Apocalyptic Imagination* notes likewise that apocalyptic "does not involve doctrinal consistency." The constant factor within it is that matters are "put in perspective by the otherworldly revelation of a transcendent world and eschatological judgment." He suggests that apocalyptic was "surely one crucial ingredient in the formation" of Christianity. It enabled Christians to understand Jesus' resurrection as "a revelatory event that provided a new perspective on life and history" that was "distinctly apocalyptic."[46] The content of the distinctly apocalyptic appears for Collins to be some view of God's coming judgment in light of which the present may be interpreted.

J. Christiaan Beker in *Paul the Apostle* also stresses the importance of apocalyptic expectation for the New Testament, but he defines the genre in a different manner from Perrin, the Society of Biblical Literature, or Collins. Beker lists three central ideas in apocalyptic: historical dualism, universal cosmic expectation, and the imminent end of the world. He asserts that "Paul's thought is anchored in the apocalyptic worldview and that the resurrection of Christ can only be understood from that setting."[47]

The main thrust of Beker's argument is that Paul's theology is informed by a specific hope for the future: the Parousia and consummation of the kingdom (Rom. 5:1-2; 8:18, 23; 1 Thess. 1:10; Gal. 5:5).[48] For Beker, the apocalyptic worldview provided Paul with categories sufficient to display the significance of Jesus' resurrection as the beginning of "the new age to come and . . . as an inherent part of the transformation and recreation of all reality in the apocalyptic age."[49]

This brief and less-than-exhaustive glance at recent biblical scholarship on Jewish and early Christian apocalyptic shows that there is no scholarly consensus on what the content of the apocalyptic genre entails, other than that it involves some orientation toward a future of God's intervention. Even that similarity is purely formal, because the content or import of such intervention is not a point of agreement in these various construals.

Given such disagreement, it is problematic to speak simply, as is often done, of a recovery or discovery of the apocalyptic shape of the New Testament in this century. Indeed, biblical scholars and theologians in recent decades have advanced numerous and often conflicting views of apocalyptic. They have not presented a lucid historical or literary reconstruction on which there is substantial agreement. These writers agree on neither what it is that they have supposedly discovered, nor on its theological and moral significance. Some interpret apocalyptic as a literary genre, while others see it as a matrix of future expectations with varying distinguishing marks.

Because of such points of disagreement, we will not critique these positions on the so-called recovery of apocalyptic nor construct a Christian eschatology thereon. That is, we will not work from a "text" of a historical-critical reconstruction of apocalyptic as a basis for making theological arguments. We do not pursue this line of thought because it is uncertain what critical insight on the New Testament has been provided by the debate on apocalyptic, other than the point that certain texts assume that Jesus of Nazareth has some unspecified relevance for the future.

It is true that hope for a future blessed by God was a prominent Old Testament theme which preceded the events surrounding Jesus of Nazareth. Yet a reconstruction of such expectation, in and of itself, does not provide a sound starting point for systematic discourse on Christian eschatology. Rolf Rendtorff describes the eschatological nature of Old Testament theology well with his statement that

> since the time of deutero-Isaiah, the coming of this [final] demonstration of Yahweh's power became the subject of eschatological hope: its final and ultimate manifestation was awaited as the most imminent and decisive experience of the endtime.[50]

But such hope for the future was not uniform in Old Testament faith. For example, the prophetic vision of Isaiah 65:17-25 brings hope for "new heavens and a new earth" in which "no more shall there be in it an infant that lives but a few days, or an old person who does not live out a lifetime." Then the "wolf and the lamb shall feed together." Amos looks forward to a time when God "will restore the fortunes of my people Israel, and they shall rebuild the ruined cities" (Amos 9:14). Ezekiel envisions a time when God "will open your graves, and bring you up from your graves . . . [and] bring you back to the land of Israel" (Ezek. 37:1-14).

The particular content of such hope, as the cited passages indicate, was quite diverse. One may grant the conclusion of scholarship on Jewish apocalyptic, that it concerned expectations for God's coming intervention in history. Yet such hope is still hardly one identifiable and coherent eschatological

scheme. While Christians believe that all these hopes are fulfilled in the risen Lord (2 Cor. 1:20), we cannot deduce the
identity or eschatological significance of the Christ simply as a
function of such a vague Old Testament matrix of hopes.

Instead, Christology, and especially Jesus' identity as the risen
Lord, should determine and shape eschatological hope. Christians see Jesus as the fulfillment of Jewish expectation, but this
fulfillment also transforms and shapes that hope. It was not obvious, for example, to many first-century Jews that Jesus was the
Messiah, the one for whom they hoped (John 1:11).

We can find something more promising for Christian eschatological discourse than a reconstruction of apocalyptic categories. This better way begins systematically with the confessed
belief that Jesus' resurrection is the source of our temporal hope
for a future consummation of the kingdom. It is promising because it focuses on the interrelation of Christian beliefs displayed by the central practices of the church as a foretaste of
God's fulfilled reign. Hence, its appropriateness for theological
construction is not tested against a dubious historical reconstruction of a first-century worldview. Instead, this approach is
tested by asking whether it illuminates the import of the future
that the church proclaims, enacts, and awaits in light of its faith
in the risen Lord.

Theological Construction

As we therefore leave the varied forms of apocalyptic to its
interpreters, we need to find the first constructive step in describing an eschatological orientation. That step is to display
how belief in Jesus' resurrection functions as a warrant for New
Testament writers and Christians today in speaking of the future
consummation of God's kingdom and in seeing the church and
the Christian life in close relation to a coming reign of God.
From this perspective we may critique the positions of figures
like Schweitzer and Bultmann.

In making this point, I first observe that a central theme in the
New Testament is the importance of belief in the resurrection
for Christian faith and the existence of the church. Paul writes
that Jesus "was declared to be Son of God with power . . . by res-

urrection from the dead" (Rom. 1:4). Peter's sermon in Acts 2 suggests that it is through Jesus' resurrection that "God has made him both Lord and Messiah, this Jesus whom you crucified" (Acts 2:36).

Likewise, the four canonical Gospels presuppose that Jesus has been raised. That event is a necessary condition for the good news that they proclaim. In Matthew's Gospel, the risen Lord gives his followers the missionary challenge to proclaim the good news, to "make disciples of all nations" (Matt. 28:19). In Mark's Gospel, the prediction of his death and resurrection is the troubling but crucial news about the kind of Messiah that Jesus would be (Mark 8:32-33). According to Luke, the risen Lord asks, "Was it not necessary that the Messiah should suffer these things and then enter into his glory?" This passage indicates that the resurrection is a necessary aspect of Jesus' identification as the Messiah, the Christ (Luke 24:26). Similarly, John's account sees the resurrection as a vital step in Jesus "leaving the world and . . . going to the Father" in glory (John 16:28). It is an event that manifests how "grace and truth came through Jesus Christ" (John 1:17).

In Romans 10:9, Paul emphasizes the centrality of Jesus' resurrection for salvation: "If you confess with your lips that Jesus is Lord and believe in your heart that God raised him from the dead, you will be saved." This salvation entails a future hope, since "we have peace with God through our Lord Jesus Christ, . . . and we boast in our hope of sharing the glory of God" (Rom. 5:1-2). That hope contextualizes the present, for "the sufferings of this present time are not worth comparing with the glory about to be revealed to us" (Rom. 8:18).

This future glory refers to the fulfillment of the resurrection process begun with God raising Jesus as "the first fruits of those who have died." His resurrection is the beginning of a sequence:

> Christ the first fruits, then at his coming those who belong to Christ. Then comes the end, when he hands over the kingdom to God the Father, after he has destroyed every ruler and every authority and power. (1 Cor. 15:23-24)

These passages indicate that, on the basis of Jesus' resurrection, Christians should look forward to the consummation of God's kingdom, to the coming of "a new heaven and a new earth" (Rev. 21:1). Jesus' raising is crucial for such expectation: "If for this life only we have hoped in Christ, we are of all people most to be pitied" (1 Cor. 15:19). As the Nicene Creed states, "We look for a resurrection of the dead, and the life of the age to come."

I am certainly not the first theologian to notice that Jesus' resurrection is described in the New Testament as an event of profound significance for the future. Jürgen Moltmann displays well the logic of temporal hope in relation to the Lord's resurrection in his *Theology of Hope: On the Ground and Implications of a Christian Eschatology.* He declares that Christian faith "lives from the raising of the crucified Christ"; therefore, hope for the future "is the medium of Christian faith as such, the key in which everything is set, the glow that suffuses everything here in the dawn of an expected day."[51]

Moltmann frames eschatological questions within the context of Jesus' resurrection because he believes that "Christian eschatology is at heart Christology in an eschatological perspective." Not simply a "Christianized [Jewish] apocalyptic," it works from the radical assumption that "the raising of the dead has already taken place" in Jesus' resurrection, and that faith in him is the guarantee of future resurrection. In this way, eschatology examines "the inner tendency of the resurrection event, asking what rightly can and must be expected from the risen and exalted Lord."[52]

Moltmann recognizes, however, that Christian belief in the significance of Jesus' resurrection for the future arose "within the special horizon of prophetic and apocalyptic expectations, hopes and questions about that which, according to the promises of this God, is to come." The diverse matrix of Jewish expectation for a future of God's reign did not rigidly control the believers' hope in the future of the risen Lord. Yet

> Christian eschatology expounded and expressed the Easter experiences in recalling and taking up the earlier promises and—in re-

gard to Jesus himself—in recalling and taking up what had earlier been promised and proclaimed. The Easter appearances are bound up with this eschatological horizon, both in that which they presuppose and call to mind and also in that which they themselves prefigure and provoke.[53]

Within this context, Moltmann identifies a key aspect of the distinctiveness of belief in the risen Jesus as the firstfruits of future resurrection. He claims that

> the raising of the dead has already taken place in this one case for all, and that the raising was performed not on one faithful to the law but on one who was crucified, and consequently future resurrection is to be expected not from obedience to the law but from the justification of sinners and from faith in Christ. The central place of the Torah in late Jewish apocalyptic is thus taken by the person and the cross of Christ.[54]

Moltmann does not systematically rely on a particular historical reconstruction of apocalyptic and formulate a view of the Christ's significance for the future in that light. Instead, he notes that hope for the future of God's reign "comes of observing a specific, unique event [Jesus' resurrection]. . . . The hopeful theological mind, however, can observe this event only in seeking to span the future horizon projected by this event." Thus theology "inquires about the mission of Christ and the intention of God in raising him from the dead," for "he must reign until he has put all his enemies under his feet" (1 Cor. 15:25).[55]

God has overcome "the god-forsakeness of God's ambassador," the annihilation of the Incarnate Word, by raising him from death. Because of this, Christians believe that God will overcome all sin and rebellion through the risen Lord, who is the firstfruits of God's coming reign.[56] On the resurrection of Jesus, Moltmann says,

> What happened to him is understood as the dawn and assured promise of the coming glory of God over all, as the victory of life from God over death. Cross and resurrection are then not merely *modi* in the person of Christ. Rather, their dialectic is an open dia-

lectic, which will find its resolving synthesis only in the eschaton of all things.[57]

In *Christian Theology: An Eschatological Approach*, Thomas N. Finger states well the importance of viewing Jesus' resurrection in this light: To apprehend the significance of Jesus' resurrection,

> theology must pause in wonder and horror before the paradox of the cross. Here the one claiming kingship suffered the torture reserved for the lowest criminals and slaves. The herald of hope died in despair. The one living in closest communion with God expired in most bitter abandonment. Until one has grasped the horrible finality of this "verdict," there can be no understanding of the triumph of the resurrection.[58]

By reflecting on the implications of God overcoming this most horrible death, Finger suggests that the first Christians saw that God had conquered sin and evil in principle. Eventually God would use the agent of their conquest, the risen Lord, to subordinate fully all things to God. Indeed, this process of final subordination had already begun. The diverse hopes of Israel for the manifestation of God's righteousness had been fulfilled in the unexpected spectacle of the resurrection of one who was crucified as a blasphemer.[59]

Wolfhart Pannenberg emphasizes in a similar way the importance of the resurrection for the beginning of a new age of God's reign in *Jesus—God and Man*: "If Jesus has been raised, then the end of the world has begun." He notes that for Paul, Jesus is "the firstborn within a large family" (Romans 8:29), raised as the firstfruits of the new age (1 Cor. 15:20). He explains that

> Jesus' claim to authority . . . was . . . blasphemous for Jewish ears. Because of this, Jesus was then also slandered by the Jews before the Roman governor as a rebel. If Jesus really has been raised, this claim has been visibly and unambiguously confirmed by the God of Israel, who was allegedly blasphemed by Jesus. This was done by Israel's God. A Jew . . . would certainly not take an event of this kind as one that came to be apart from the will of God. That the primitive Christian proclamation in fact understood Jesus' resur-

rection from the dead as the confirmation of his pre-Easter claim emerges above all in the speeches in Acts.[60]

In this way, there is an "inherent significance" in Jesus' resurrection within the context of Jewish "expectation for the future."[61] For the first Christians, eschatological hope came to focus on the future of the one who was crucified as a blasphemer and then raised up and vindicated by God.

> After Jesus' resurrection it must have become meaningless to expect a second figure in addition to him with the same function and the same mode of coming. By virtue of the resurrection, Jesus had moved into the role of the Son of Man.[62]

Pannenberg proposes that

> through the resurrection, the revealer of God's eschatological will became the incarnation of the eschatological reality itself; the ultimate revelation of God's will for humanity and for the whole of creation could therefore be expected of him.[63]

Pannenberg thinks that there is no reason within the context of New Testament proclamation or Jewish expectation to view Jesus as the Christ or Son of Man apart from his resurrection understood as the beginning of the fulfillment of God's kingdom. He insists that "when one discusses the truth of the apocalyptic expectation of a future judgment and a resurrection of the dead, one is dealing directly with the basis of Christian faith." In other words,

> Why the man Jesus can be the ultimate revelation of God, why in him and only in him God is supposed to have appeared, remains incomprehensible apart from the horizon of the apocalyptic expectation.[64]

Pannenberg's use of the term *apocalyptic* may reflect the assumption that the term has a precise meaning established by historical-critical research. Nevertheless, he does rightly make the point that belief in Jesus' resurrection as the beginning of the consummation of God's kingdom arose within a matrix of Jewish expectations. Within that matrix Jesus played an unexpected and transforming role as the "blasphemer" who was raised from the dead. Hence, all of Israel's hopes for a future blessed by God will be fulfilled in him.[65]

In seeking greater clarity on the nature of this temporal expectation in light of the risen Lord, it is helpful to turn to Walter Kasper. In *Jesus the Christ*, he makes the comment that Christian faith does not espouse simply some unspecified hope for the future.

> Jesus' Resurrection signifies an adjustment of the apocalyptic worldview: an adjustment which means in fact that the New Testament concept is not one of any particular future for the world, but has to do with the future of Jesus Christ. What it has in mind is the universal extension of what was ultimately apparent in Jesus as a person and in his destiny.[66]

Kasper's point is insightful. Crucial to belief in Jesus' eschatological significance is his particular identity as a Jew who proclaimed God's kingdom in an unexpected way, was killed as a blasphemer and a rebel, and was raised from the dead. God vindicates him in spite of an ignominious death, and Jesus' resurrection identifies him as the Son whose raising foretells the destiny of all reality for God's redemption and final blessing.

Kasper continues:

> Jesus' resurrection means more than the final acceptance and confirmation of Jesus and his reception into community of life and love of God. In the Resurrection and Exaltation of Jesus, God also accepted Jesus' existence for others and finally established peace and reconciliation with the world. In and through Jesus, God's love is now finally addressed to all men [and women].[67]

Such love and reconciliation will find their fulfillment in the coming consummation of the kingdom, which Christians see as the extension of the overcoming of death, sin, and alienation worked in the resurrection of Jesus.

In other words, Kasper points us toward a Christocentric view of God's coming reign. Following his systematic point, Christians should approach eschatology by asking: What may we expect for the future in light of the risen Lord? We should work from belief in the risen Lord to speak of the future, not from some prior commitment about the future to speak of Jesus' relevance.[68]

In a way similar to Kasper, Jon Sobrino in *Christology at the Crossroads* focuses on the raising of Jesus. He claims that a view of one person's resurrection as the beginning of a universal resurrection or a new age is unique to Christianity among the larger circle of so-called apocalyptic movements (1 Thess. 4:14-17; 1 Cor. 15:51).[69] Sobrino thinks that a common element in the diverse genre of Jewish apocalyptic expectation and Christian hope is that they both expect "the vindication of God's justice." He emphasizes, however, that the gospel is uniquely the good news of the resurrection of God's Messiah, the vindication of the Son who is the particular human Jesus of Nazareth, not the raising of just anybody.[70]

The force of Sobrino's point is intensified when we remember that the particular human Jesus of Nazareth hardly fit the predominant expectations for the Messiah of Israel. He did not call for the stringent observance of the law or working the liberation of the Jews from Rome. Instead, he was far from a stickler for the religious laws of his day and nonresistantly accepted death at the hands of the imperial authorities.[71] The gospel is the good news of God's raising of this unexpected Messiah, who was rejected by his own people and killed in the lowliest fashion. Christian eschatology is grounded in the future of *this* humiliated but now risen Lord.

Thus Moltmann, Finger, Pannenberg, Kasper, and Sobrino highlight the significance of Jesus' resurrection in a way that is convincing and fits the New Testament texts. I therefore follow them in emphasizing that a Christocentric temporal hope for the coming consummation of God's kingdom is a central component of Christian belief.[72] This hope is for the future fulfillment of the new age begun in Jesus' resurrection, the age of resurrection and subordination to God that Christians expect because of God's raising of the crucified Messiah (1 Cor. 15:20-28). The orientations of these theologians are rightly Christocentric on this point. They demonstrate that the new age of God's justice for which Christians hope is precisely the future reign of the God incarnate in Jesus. The kingdom is not the domain of an unknown deity or of a God who could be known fully before or apart from the life, death, and resurrection of this particular human being. Instead, the kingdom for which Christians hope is the completion of the justice embodied in our Lord's ministry and resurrection.

For Christians, the risen Lord is the key to, and the guarantee of, the eschatological destiny of all reality to be in subjection to God. The risen Jesus is the source and ground of our hope for the fulfillment of the new age. His raising from death has begun a sequence of resurrection that will culminate in the fullness of God's reign (1 Cor. 15:20-28). Through the resurrection of Jesus, God overcame the obscene spectacle of the killing of the Messiah as a blasphemer and rebel. In the light of that triumph, Christians believe that God will one day overcome all evil and rebellion through the agency of the risen Lord. God's conquest of evil on Easter morning is the guarantee of the Almighty's final victory.

Church As Foretaste of the New Age

The church, when viewed in this eschatological perspective, is well described as a foretaste of the coming kingdom. It is a community of the new age begun in Jesus' resurrection, a community which proleptically and imperfectly embodies God's rule. The key aspect of this identification is the presence of the Holy Spirit with the church as the power and sign of God's reign.

In central New Testament texts, it is only after the ascension of the risen Lord that Joel's prophecy is fulfilled: "In the last days it will be, God declares, that I will pour out my Spirit upon all flesh" (Acts 2:17; Joel 2:28-32). The Spirit comes to the church after the risen Lord's ascension: "The Holy Spirit . . . will teach you everything, and remind you of all that I have said to you" (John 14:26). It is through Pentecost that the God incarnate in Jesus of Nazareth becomes present with the church through the gift of the Spirit. If Pentecost were not temporally located after Jesus' resurrection and ascension, it would be unintelligible as the founding of the church of Jesus Christ.[73]

French L. Arrington explores the significance of the presence of the Spirit in *Paul's Aeon Theology in 1 Corinthians*. He notes that Paul understands Jesus to have become "a life-giving spirit" in the resurrection (1 Cor. 15:45); now "the present work of [the risen] Christ is pneumatic." The Spirit and the risen Lord are so closely linked for Paul that "the present possession of Spirit is interchangeable with 'Christ in you, the hope of glory.' " Through the presence of the Spirit, "Paul sees the eschatological power of God as already operative in 'this age.' Indeed, for him the Spirit is the chief mark that the new age is dawning."[74]

This new age of "the kingdom does not consist in words, but in power," a notion that is synonymous with the presence and action of the Spirit, for example, in Jesus' resurrection (Rom. 1:4; 1 Cor. 4:20). The fullness of that power will be revealed when "the Lord comes, who will bring to light the things now hidden. . . . Then each one will receive commendation from God" (1 Cor. 4:5). In this way, the presence of the Spirit of the risen Lord is a sign of the new age which Jesus' resurrection has begun. It is this presence which enables the church to be an eschatological community, a proleptic manifestation of God's kingdom.

Gerhard Lohfink in *Jesus and Community* makes the complementary exegetical point that

> the coming of God's Spirit is an eschatological phenomenon. The Spirit is described as God's gift to the eschatological community, and even as God's power which truly creates eschatological Israel (cf. Isa. 32:15; Ezek. 11:19; 36:26-27; 37:14; Joel 3:1-2).[75]

Hence, miracles in the first Christian communities were "not to be described only as accompanying legitimate signs of the presence of the Spirit" (Gal. 3:1-5).[76] Instead, the presence of gifts of the Spirit indicated that

> God's eschatological Spirit had already been poured out; he was already active in the communities in a multiplicity of charisms.

> Where Jesus spoke of the presence of the reign of God, the early church spoke of the presence of the Spirit. The language thus changed as a result of the experience after Easter. But the basic line of Jesus' message was continued. The future of eschatological salvation had already begun.[77]

Lohfink's argument is persuasive because he indicates that the Spirit who is present with the church is precisely the Spirit of the risen Lord, whose raising is the beginning of God's new age. This point demonstrates how the risen Lord's promise, "I am with you always, to the end of the age," is validated by the coming of the Spirit at Pentecost (Matt. 28:20). As that Lord is now present with the church through the gift of the Spirit, the church is empowered and challenged to become the proleptic social location of God's kingdom. Through the Spirit, the Messiah is with the church.

The church, then, has the task of proleptically embodying the kingdom by following its Lord in the sort of faithfulness that all reality will display when "all things are subjected to him" in the eschaton (1 Cor. 15:26-28). That difficult task of the church becomes a central focus of Christian ethics: to guide the embodiment of proper faithfulness to the risen Lord in the time between Pentecost and Parousia.

The church's observance of the Lord's Supper and baptism reflects how this eschatological location has direct relevance for the Christian life. The performance of these ecclesial practices demands the church's faithfulness as an expression of our hope for the fullness of the new age begun in Jesus' resurrection.

The Supper is an eschatological meal whereby we "proclaim the Lord's death until he comes" (1 Cor. 11:26). We celebrate in light of his future, and we anticipate the fullness of that future. Carl Braaten puts it well in *The Future of God:* the Supper

> is a miniature meal eaten together in anticipation of the messianic banquet. . . . Holy Communion is a prolepsis of the final rendezvous of all the separated in the world to come.[78]

By taking the Supper, Christians are called to live in a manner appropriate to the future which we proclaim in our eating and drinking. We locate ourselves in an eschatological context in which the service of the risen Lord becomes the proper goal of human life.

Similarly, in baptism we are "buried with him . . . so that, just as Christ was raised from the dead by the glory of the Father, so we too might walk in newness of life" (Rom. 6:4). Baptism is a practice through which we participate proleptically in the resurrection that the consummated kingdom will bring. We are called, by virtue of our baptism, to follow Jesus in the life of the new age *in the here and now.*

Through the practices of the Lord's Supper and baptism, the church symbolically foreshadows God's coming kingdom. The community of faith thereby demonstrates and proclaims the centrality of hope in God's coming reign that is demanded by faith in the risen Lord. By performing these practices, Christians are called to discern what faithfulness to the risen Lord entails in their particular circumstances.

The following three statements indicate the basic significance of this view of the relationship between eschatology and ethics: (1) Jesus' resurrection has begun a new age of resurrection and faithfulness to the demands of God's reign, which has not yet been consummated. (2) The gift of the Spirit at Pentecost empowers the church to manifest a foretaste of the fulfillment of this new age. (3) A central task of Christian ethics is providing guidance for living as part of the faith community in a manner appropriate to this new age.

In this way of proceeding, eschatology shapes church and ethics in the sense of locating them within the temporal horizon of the consummation of the kingdom. Church and the Christian life become, then, realities between Pentecost and Parousia. They are forward-looking, hopeful endeavors which await and anticipate the coming kingdom of God. The resurrection of Jesus is the ground for "our hope of sharing the glory of God" while we look for the Parousia and the consummation of God's kingdom (Rom. 5:2). Thus eschatological hope is not an isolated aspect of Christian belief; it shapes and locates ecclesiology and ethics as matters between the times of Pentecost and Parousia.

A Distinctive Approach

Much is at stake theologically and morally in the eschatological issues discussed above. To demonstrate this claim, we will briefly engage the views of the relationship between eschatology and ethics advanced by Weiss, Schweitzer, Dodd, Bultmann, and Wilder. A common problematic trait of each of these approaches is an attempt to discern the significance of Jesus primarily as a moral teacher. Their views virtually ignore his identity as the risen Lord, which is a crucial aspect of Christian belief.

The issue which they seek to address is that the Gospels portray Jesus making statements about a coming reign that apparently did not come to pass. Jesus even interprets his entire ministry as part of that reign. Hence, Weiss, Schweitzer, Bultmann, and Wilder agree that Jesus was simply wrong. Weiss, Bultmann, and Wilder search for various perspectives from which to interpret Jesus' preaching in a way that will rescue its moral relevance. They properly assume that the last word on Jesus for Christians simply cannot be that he was profoundly mistaken! Dodd, on the other hand, denies that the kingdom proclaimed by Jesus was primarily a future reality; he thereby attempts to avoid the theological problems associated with Jesus' supposedly mistaken predictions.

Their strategies are inadequate, however, because they fail to interpret the Gospels' portraits of Jesus' ministry in light of his resurrection as the beginning of the new age of God's kingdom that he proclaimed. Put another way, they each assume that Jesus' primary relevance is as a preacher of the kingdom, a teacher of the morality appropriate to God's reign. They fail to give systematic primacy to Jesus' postresurrection identity as the risen Lord, who is present with the church since Pentecost and has cosmic and ultimate redemptive significance.

It is helpful to examine the underlying historicist assumptions of these views of "Jesus as preacher." To bracket Jesus' resurrection and separate it from discourse on his moral significance, in order to attend purely to his preaching, is to place him within the historical category of moral or perhaps "apocalyptic" teachers. One thus describes and interprets him in line with a preestablished notion of how he could be morally significant and of what it means to be morally significant.

Moltmann forces the issue well in his statement:

> The concept of the historical, of the historically possible and the historically probable, has been developed in the modern age on the basis of experiences of history other than the experience of the raising of Jesus from the dead—namely, since the Enlightenment, on the basis of the experience of [the hu]man's ability to calculate history and to make it. The controversy between the disciples and the Jews was concerned with the question: has God raised him from the dead according to the promises, or can God according to his promises not have raised him? The modern controversy on the resurrection, however, is concerned with the question whether resurrection is historically possible.[79]

Moltmann explains that a usual requirement for the description of something as historical is some point of analogy to what has happened before. This comparison establishes sufficient similarity to other events to enable a categorization in accord with previous experience.[80] Within such an interpretative context, "the assertion of a raising of Jesus by God appears as a myth concerning a supernatural incursion which is contradicted by all our experience of the world."[81]

A common factor in these views is the description of Jesus' significance according to the historical standards of how a first-century preacher could be significant in the twentieth century. That is, they seek to find a way to interpret his teachings so that they have some relevance for people who can see in retrospect that he was wrong about the coming of God's reign.

Thus Jesus' kingdom expectation is theologically embarrassing to these theologians and must be made systematically unimportant for their constructive work in Christian ethics. Reliance on Jesus' resurrection as a determining aspect of his present significance would be unacceptable because it would challenge their desire to portray Jesus in a morally congenial light to modernist, historicist sensibilities. Persons with such an outlook do not know what to make of talk about someone overcoming death; that talk contradicts the assumptions of modernity.[82]

Moltmann points toward the construction of an alternative to these views:

> The resurrection of Christ is without parallel in the history known to us. But it can for that very reason be regarded as a "history-making event" in the light of which all other history is illumined, called in question, and transformed. . . . Then the resurrection of Christ does not offer itself as an analogy to that which can be experienced any time and anywhere, but as an analogy to what is to come to all.'. . . . It is to be called historic because, by pointing the way for future events, it makes history in which we can and must live. It is historic, because it discloses an eschatological future.[83]

Such talk of a real temporal future of God's reign created by Jesus' resurrection is, of course, absent from the construals of Weiss, Schweitzer, Dodd, Bultmann, and Wilder. By failing to reckon with the significance of Jesus' resurrection for the future, they have failed to display a central aspect of Christian belief which is profoundly important for both ecclesiology and ethics.

If one lacks such Christocentric eschatological convictions, it is hard to see in what sense the church may be a foretaste of the new age through the power of the Spirit in anticipation of God's fulfilled reign. One would even wonder why the church should be of much concern as a distinct, identifiable community of discipleship. It is difficult, likewise, to know what it would mean to "proclaim the Lord's death until he comes" in the Lord's Supper without a temporal context that makes the reference to the future intelligible (1 Cor. 11:26).

Over against such nontemporal construals, I think that it is precisely because Christ is risen and present with the church through the Spirit as a sign of the new age that the faith community gains a critical perspective on the world. Believers see a world that is not yet part of the fulfilled reign of God as the domain of the risen Lord and destined for right subjection to God. In other words, Jesus' identity as the risen Lord is of great importance for the theological description of the Christian life and of the world itself.

Our approach is unlike Schweitzer, for whom Jesus is "a

stranger and an enigma" whose ministry was based on wrong assumptions about the future. Instead, we suggest that Christians should see Jesus, who has been raised from the dead, as the hope of the world for salvation, and indeed the hope of all reality for salvation.[84] The risen Lord has cosmological, universal significance as the one who "must reign until he has put all his enemies under his feet" (1 Cor. 15:25).

On the basis of such universal claims, Christian eschatology has direct relevance for the description of the world as a realm destined for God's final salvation. The second person of the Trinity is the agent of both creation and redemption (John 1:3; Col. 1:15-20). The Christ is both "the Alpha and the Omega, the first and the last, the beginning and the end" (Rev. 22:12-13; cf. 1:8). The destiny of the world, as foreshadowed in the risen Lord, is for subjection to God. Therefore, ethics should concern the eschatologically shaped task of describing the significance of human behavior in accord with the destiny of all reality, including humanity, for future subordination to God. Given that destiny, Christians believe that all humans should become disciples of the risen Lord and follow the Christ who is the key to the future of the universe. Since the resurrection has begun God's new age, Christians must live in a manner appropriate to this new order.

An assumption of this approach is that only with belief in Jesus' resurrection may Christians discern rightly the significance of Jesus and of the kingdom that he proclaimed. Indeed, his identity as the risen Lord must be incorporated systematically into any assessment of who Jesus is and of what it would mean to be faithful to him. God has vindicated Jesus through resurrection and has made him present with the church through the gift of the Spirit at Pentecost. Hence, it is problematic to limit consideration of Jesus' relevance to his earthly ministry in a fashion that ignores his resurrection and its implications. Indeed, it was by resurrection that he "was declared the Son of God" (Romans 1:4).

If Jesus were simply a deceased rabbi who had wrongly predicted God's coming reign, Schweitzer likely would be correct in his description of him primarily as a stranger without direct relevance for the moral life. However, Christians believe that Jesus' resurrection was a sign that guaranteed God's future triumph over all evil and began the fulfillment of the kingdom which Jesus proclaimed. Hence, Schweitzer's formulation is wholly inadequate. It obscures Jesus' identity as the risen Lord, in whose future lies the destiny of all reality and who is now present with the church through the Spirit.

Moreover, Schweitzer's view makes the significance of Jesus depend on the assumption that God's kingdom has not begun in his resurrection and that a new age of salvation has not been ushered in with the Lord's raising. If the last word on Jesus is that he wrongly expected the kingdom to come, Christians are wrong in seeing the world as a realm that he will redeem. Belief in Jesus' resurrection is a systematically crucial affirmation of Christian theology.[85]

Our way of construing the significance of eschatology for ethics is distinct, likewise, from that of Weiss. He makes a futuristic eschatology irrelevant for the moral life and returns to a timeless ethical view of the kingdom. Instead, we insist on the importance of the temporal location of the Christian life as an endeavor between Pentecost and Parousia.[86] The following of Jesus is by definition eschatological because Jesus' resurrection has begun a new age which will find fulfillment in the future. The Spirit is present with the church to enable its manifestation of a foretaste of that coming fulfillment. The Christian life occurs between Pentecost and Parousia, which are temporal reference points without which the Christian faith would be unintelligible.

Our perspective contrasts with Weiss's view that Christianity sustains an invisible commonwealth of moral agents. It is more appropriate to see the church as an identifiable social order which is located eschatologically by the future which it proleptically embodies through the power of the Spirit.[87] Indeed, the very existence of the church depends upon the claim that the Lord is risen and present with his followers, that Jesus' significance for the Christian life may not be discerned rightly apart from his resurrection understood as the beginning of a new age.

Moreover, if we view Jesus primarily as a preacher of erroneous expectations about the future, we obscure the unique identity of the church as a foretaste of the new age. Such a detour would emphasize "Jesus as confused teacher" over "Jesus as risen Lord," and it would make Christian eschatological discourse a dubious undertaking. If the only basis for such expectation is Jesus' assumed-to-be-wrong teaching, then there is no compelling warrant for a Christian eschatology. Hence, there would be no basis for speaking of the church as an eschatological reality. In this respect, Weiss's rejection of eschatology is of a piece with his talk of an invisible moral community. Without such eschatological expectation, it is hard to see why one particular social grouping, the church, could embody proleptically God's new age or be of any great moral interest.

Our critique of Bultmann and Wilder is similar. They see the expectation for a future reign as a piece of antiquated Jewish mythology which cloaked Jesus' real concern for obedience to the will of God in every moment. Their views of eschatology and ethics take Jesus' futuristic expectation as wrong. Then they seek some way to sustain his moral relevance by identifying an existentialist kernel hidden within the eschatological husk. Thus they operate under the dubious theological assumption that Jesus' resurrection is unimportant for understanding the sense in which he has initiated God's kingdom. Indeed, they interpret talk of a future kingdom in a fashion which denies its temporal nature.[88]

Bultmann and Wilder describe the situation as though there is, on one hand, Jesus' incorrect expectation and, on the other, a static world for which Jesus' teaching must be made relevant. Hence, they interpret the kingdom expectation in a fashion that makes its meaning compatible with contemporary worldviews, such as an existentialism that calls for self-actualization through living each moment as though it were "the last hour."[89] Eschatology drops out of the picture except as a medium for the expression of other views which are more congenial for moderns who do not expect a future reign of God. Instead of revising contemporary worldviews in light of the future created by Jesus' resurrection, they construe references in the New Testament to a temporal hope for the kingdom in accord with nontemporal hermeneutical assumptions.

Given the basic assertion of Christian faith that Jesus' resurrection has begun a new age, this discussion shows that the Christian life is temporally located in a fundamental sense. It is contextualized by a series of events that will culminate in the fullness of God's kingdom. Since Jesus is the risen Lord of the world, the moral life properly concerns pursuing faithfulness to this Messiah in and through a community of his disciples which seeks to display partially the future of God's reign. Hence, it follows that eschatological expectation should shape and determine the description of Christian ethics: it is not simply a rhetorical strategy to call for obedience or self-actualization in a nontemporal framework.

In addition, our approach to ethics does not have the primarily individualistic slant of Bultmann and Wilder. Instead, the Christian life is contextualized by its social nature as an undertaking in the community that, through the power of the Spirit, foreshadows God's reign.[90] Ethics concerns the guiding of human behavior as part of a creation which is destined for God's full redemption, not primarily the purity of the will of the individual. Each person is a human moral agent and is described fundamentally as part of a cosmic process of God's salvation. The individual human being, however, is one aspect of that process, not the conceptual center of the moral life. The social reality of the church as a foretaste of the kingdom, not the individual, becomes the entity of greatest material interest for Christian ethics.

Likewise, it is necessary to criticize Dodd for failing to appreciate the sense in which the kingdom, though initiated in Jesus' ministry and resurrection, awaits its fulfillment in the future.[91] Like the other figures whom we have engaged, Dodd made the error of constructing an eschatology primarily on the basis of Jesus' teachings without sufficient attention to the significance of his resurrection for the future of God's reign.

Dodd sought to sustain Jesus' moral relevance for the twentieth century by portraying the kingdom as a timeless realm present in his ministry and by denying that he wrongly expected a coming kingdom. Through Dodd's approach, however, he obscures the temporal location of the Christian life between Pentecost and Parousia. No less than the other figures, Dodd fails to convey the basic claim of Christian belief that Jesus' resurrection has begun a new age, not yet completely fulfilled, in which disciples must pursue a communally sustained faithfulness in the midst of a rebellious world.

The perspectives of Schweitzer, Weiss, Dodd, Bultmann, and Wilder, then, share a common error. They construct eschatologies and views of the kingdom's relevance for the moral life which are not informed by Jesus' resurrection as the beginning of a new age, as the guarantee of the temporal future of God's kingdom.

This volume develops a position distinct from their formulations. It reflects more adequately the descriptive relevance of Christian faith for selected matters of the moral life by working out certain theological and ethical implications of Jesus' identity as the risen Lord. The resurrection of Jesus, when viewed in proper eschatological context, affects how we understand the church, how we think about what discipleship entails, and how we respond to those who think that discipleship requires a moral retreat from the real problems of life in the world. Our discussion will show that eschatology has a profound and coherent influence for Christian ethics.

Church As Proleptic Social Locus of the New Age

The church is empowered by the presence of the Spirit as a foretaste of the new age begun in Jesus' resurrection. This view of eschatology as hope in the future of the risen Lord leads naturally to consideration of the social or ecclesial nature of the Christian life.[1] It forces a practical question: What must the church be and do in order to exist in a manner appropriate to its temporal location between Pentecost and Parousia?

This chapter outlines a way to respond to that question. At a conceptual level, our discussion identifies certain conditions of the social realization of a community which manifests through the power of the Spirit a communal discipleship or imitation of Christ in a manner appropriate to its eschatological location.

Toward the Social Production of the Church

In thinking about what it would mean for a church to embody proleptically God's new age, it is helpful to engage aspects of the work of both John Howard Yoder and Michel Foucault. Yoder and Foucault may appear as strange conversation partners; their projects have in many respects quite different thrusts.

Yoder writes as a confessing Christian on theology and ethics.[2] Throughout his publications, he stresses the peculiar eschatological identity of the church as a proleptic social manifestation of God's reign: "The church is called to be now what the world is called to be ultimately."[3] He teaches that the community of faith is to sustain the pursuit of discipleship as a "messianic ethic" which makes the life of Jesus of Nazareth "normative for a contemporary Christian social ethic."[4] Yoder seeks to hold moral claims accountable to the gospel:

> The church precedes the world epistemologically. We know more fully from Jesus Christ and in the context of the confessed faith than we know in other ways.[5]

In contrast, Foucault dismisses ontological claims about the nature of reality through a method of "genealogy, . . . a form of history which can account for the constitution of knowledges, discourses, [and] domains of objects" without reference to the seemingly abstract enterprise of theology.[6] Foucault rejects notions of human nature and other essentialist claims by a radical historicism which locates them within matrices of power and regulation that amount to the standard according to which truth claims are advanced. He argues that

> truth is a thing of this world: it is produced only by virtue of multiple forms of constraint. [It concerns] "the ensemble of rules according to which the true and the false are separated and specific effects of power attached to the true." [Hence, the political problem] is not changing people's consciousness . . . but the political, economic, institutional regime of the production of truth.[7]

Foucault insists that standards of truth are the products of socially embodied forces of power in society. Hence, analysis of intellectual positions may not remain at the level of pure theory; it must grapple with the forces and interests of its production.

Yoder understands himself to be working out the implications of Christian belief for the life of the church. Foucault, however, seeks to identify the conditions of the intelligibility and production of beliefs and claims. He would reject Yoder's theological claims about the nature of reality in order to focus purely on their function within a social matrix. He would see Yoder as a metaphysician whose faith commitments preclude him from appreciating the social, historical nature of truth claims. In return, Yoder would see Foucault as a philosopher who describes the world as though Jesus were not the Christ. He would contend that Foucault, by failing to contextualize the particulars of history and social structures within God's creation, is precluded from seeing the meaning or purpose of history and society.[8]

Despite such profound disagreements, some of these arguments are helpful for the development of our discussion. We employ aspects of the work of both Yoder and Foucault for describing the production of the church as an eschatological community, a foretaste of the new age begun in Jesus' resurrection. The point of similarity that enables this move is their mutual rejection of theoreticism.

Foucault critiques theory by displaying its function in a given social matrix as a way of demonstrating that truth is not a matter of pure thought. Instead, truth relies on standards produced in power structures. Truth never concerns the ideal pursuit of an essence: it is "a thing of this world."[9]

Similarly, Yoder rejects the view that Christian ethics must operate in conformity to abstract conceptions of moral theory which have a basis outside the lived experience of the community of faith. He is

> skeptical about the possibility that such [an ideal metaethical] exercise could come first logically, chronologically, or developmentally. . . . What must replace the prolegomenal search for "scratch" is the confession of rootedness in historical community.[10]

This rootedness is not simply a matter of intellectual indebtedness to earlier theological affirmations. It reflects a mode of practical reason informed by the procedures and practices of the church as an identifiable social order.[11] That particular order is the locus of the production of Yoder's theological claims.

Yoder wants to hold theological discourse accountable to the embodied praxis of the community of faith, while Foucault seeks to examine all discourse in light of its social location. Despite their differences, both thinkers describe theory in the critical light of historical structures.

Yoder and Foucault's emphases on the location of theory within such structures, which are articulated in profoundly different ways in their respective projects, may serve to illuminate the eschatologically warranted identity of the church as the social locus of the Christian life. Their mutual stress on the concretely social directs attention to the practical endeavor of sustaining the church as a foretaste of the new age through a communal praxis of active faithfulness to the risen Lord. Church and ethics become, therefore, matters of social embodiment and sustenance, not theoretical notions independent of or intelligible apart from a communal context.

The first step in advancing this argument is to show how Yoder's eschatology shapes his view of the church in a way that displays the communal shape of Christian ethics. In *The Politics of Jesus*, Yoder maintains that the eschatological realm

> which Jesus proclaims is not the end of time, pure event without duration, unconnected to either yesterday or tomorrow. The jubilee is precisely an institution whose functioning within history will have a precise, practicable, limited impact. It is not a perpetual social earthquake rendering impossible any continuity of temporal effort, but a periodic revision permitting new beginnings.[12]

Yoder points to the importance of a visible, socially embodied church for the production of disciples:

> The kingdom of God is a social order and not a hidden one. . . . It is that concrete jubilary obedience . . . opening up the real accessibility of a new order in which grace and justice are linked, which men [and women] have only to accept. It does not assume time will end tomorrow; it reveals why it is meaningful that history should go on at all.[13]

Yoder's hint here that the kingdom amounts to history's hope and future ties in well with his emphasis on the political nature of the Christian life. That future is the universal subjection to

God that the church, as the social locus of discipleship, is called to manifest presently. It is the political manifestation of the new age begun in Jesus' resurrection.

This temporal eschatological location contextualizes the communal shape of Christian ethics. As Yoder suggests in *The Christian Witness to the State*, the church exists as an embodied demonstration of God's kingdom and is responsible for fidelity to its identity. In this way, the

> church is not fundamentally a source of moral stimulus to encourage the development of a better society—though a faithful church should also have this effect—it is for the sake of the church's own work that society continues to function.[14]

Hence, history's meaning "lies in the creation and work of the church" as a witness to God's salvation. This claim implies that the church's

> very existence, the fraternal relations of her members, their ways of dealing with their differences and their needs are, or rather should be, a demonstration of what love means in social relations.[15]

The church is, for Yoder, to be a political order, "a truer, more properly ordered community than is the state" due to its present willing service of God. Against alienating "hierarchical structures of authorities in pagan societies," the church should manifest an egalitarian order that provides a stark contrast to the dominant powers. Indeed, "it was the Christian community's experience of the equal dignity of every member of the congregation which ultimately . . . laid the groundwork for modern conceptions of the rights of man [and woman]."

A similarly important aspect of the church's political life is its "sober realism about the temptations of power and the persistence of sin in the life even of the righteous." Yoder suggests that faithful Christians have always

> insisted on the need for mutual fraternal admonition and especially for vigilance to be exercised by the entire congregation with regard to the faithfulness of its leaders.[16]

That vigilance is sustained through an insistence on decision making through

> a convinced consensus arrived at freely as the result of common study with the fellowship of believers. The Holy Spirit is the possession not of a few particularly gifted individuals, but of the congregation at large. [Hence, the church is essentially] a host of people called laymen [and laywomen] . . . whose primary contact with and witness to society is constituted by the fact that they earn their living and raise their families right in the midst of that society.[17]

Because of their convictions, Christians will refuse to participate in some patterns of behavior which are endorsed by the dominant culture. There is also "conscientious participation" in the projects of the larger society "by virtue of which the Christian will assist in the solution of problems and the creation of a healthy social order."[18]

In *The Priestly Kingdom*, Yoder describes some additional distinctive marks of congregational social orders which display right subordination to God. The first concerns procedures for reconciliation within the community. Following Matthew 18:15-18, he claims that

> a transcendent moral ratification is claimed for the decisions made in the conversation of two or three or more, in a context of forgiveness and in the juridical form of listening to the several witnesses.[19]

The text presents "a kind of situation ethics, . . . a procedure for doing practical moral reasoning, in a context of conflict, right in the situation where divergent views are being lived out in such a way as to cause offense." The procedure is contextualized by its ecclesial location: members prod one another in a forgiving fashion to live faithfully as disciples within an eschatological context.

Yoder thinks that to display more fully how this approach to ethics works "we need to ask not how ideas work but how the community works."[20] While every member of the community has a distinctive place in its life, he identifies a few necessary agents.

First, he identifies "Agents of Direction," who speak prophetically to provide "a vision of the place of the believing community in history, which vision locates moral reasoning" (1 Cor. 14:3, 29). The validity of such speech is judged by the community under the guidance of the Spirit.[21] Also, there are "Agents of Memory," who speak as servants of the community and its shared memory. "Scripture is the collective scribal memory," the primary substance of the memory to be tapped for guidance in the present.[22] "Agents of Linguistic Self-Consciousness" will "watch out for the sophomoric temptation of verbal distinctions without substantial necessity, and of purely verbal solutions to substantial problems." This agent will be a teacher of the community in matters of faithfulness.[23] "Agents of Order and Due Process" will ensure that "everyone else is heard, and that the conclusions reached are genuinely consensual" in the community.[24]

The starting point of ethics for Yoder is "the communal context" in terms of which various forms of moral reasoning will be pursued.[25] He wants "to attend more carefully to the agencies of a shared discerning process" than to decisionist sensibilities which reflect certain inadequacies of individualistic accounts of the moral life.[26]

Instead of focusing on metaethical distinctions, "the task of the teacher will rather be . . . to contribute to the community's awareness that every decision includes elements of principle, elements of character and due process, and elements of utility."[27] The guiding norm of discernment is "that recorded experience of practical moral reasoning in genuine human form that bears the name Jesus." Variety of ethical theory is acceptable, so long as diverse construals display the requirements of discipleship in particular instances.[28]

Yoder's description of procedures that sustain communal faithfulness ends with a provocative remark: "The only way to see how this will work will be to see how it will work."[29] By that claim, he seeks to avoid the temptation of articulating a sophisticated theory of discipleship which would take precedence over the embodied experience and practical wisdom of communities which strive to live under the guidance of the Spirit through communal moral formation.

At this point a critical appropriation of Foucault's social production orientation is helpful for spelling out the implications of Yoder's project. Foucault reminds us that standards of truth and goals of formation amount to forms of regulation, constraint, and power. The communal procedures described by Yoder fit well within this designation: they are practices which seek to structure the life and thought of the community. Yoder is suggesting that, for the church to be a distinct community which forms people with the unique moral identity of disciple, it must establish communal procedures, regulations, and structures sufficient to train its members to grow in discipleship. An implication of his approach is that communal standards of truth must be produced within socially realized patterns of faithfulness which manifest the service of God. In the midst of a rebellious world in which the church is always less than perfect, that is no mean task.

Hendrik Berkhof in *Christ and the Powers* addresses the church's struggle for faithfulness in his claim that in a rebellious world "no longer do the powers bind man [and woman] and God together; they separate them." The social structures that "undergird human life and society and preserve them from chaos" are presently distorted, serving evil and not good.[30] Berkhof suggests that it is the task of the church to demonstrate in its common life how people

> can live freed from the powers. We can only preach the manifold wisdom of God to Mammon if our life displays that we are joyfully freed from his clutches. . . . We shall only resist social injustice and the disintegration of community if justice and mercy prevail in our common life and social differences have lost their power to divide.[31]

The task of displaying the ways in which this resistance may be produced or actualized is difficult, for it requires social embodiment in community; it is not a matter of pure theory. We therefore need an account of the communal praxis which may sustain the church's resistance. In other words, we need to find a way of articulating conceptually what resistance to a sinful world requires.

This praxis develops through the habituation entailed by performing practices which may challenge dominant activities and structures of the rebellious world.[32] Through such culturally critical practices, the church may be sustained as a proleptic social manifestation of the kingdom.

The distorted social powers described by Berkhof are part of the structures and forces of a rebellious creation. They include what Foucault identified as the dominant forms of constraint and regulation which order people's lives in ways that do not manifest the service of God. This recognition warrants describing the shape of Christian moral formation between Pentecost and Parousia as believers' resistance to those disobedient forces. They resist by means of practices which sustain the community as a foretaste of the new age begun in Jesus' resurrection.

It is important to define precisely how these practices are to be understood. Such a practice is any action that manifests or sustains the church as a proleptic social manifestation of God's reign. The Spirit present with the church since Pentecost is precisely the Spirit of the risen Jesus. Hence, the practices the church is called to perform are in continuity with his call to the disciples to perform observable actions such as literally following Jesus around (Mark 1:18), healing the sick, and preaching the gospel (Luke 9:1-6). Similarly, Paul admonishes his readers to produce identifiable actions of faithfulness in, for example, the calls to refuse conformity to the world in Romans 12 and to abstain from sexual immorality in 1 Thessalonians 4:1-8. The point is that through its actions the church is to pursue a communal discipleship of active faithfulness to the risen Lord. It will thereby have enacted and embodied resources for manifesting God's reign.

The practices of the Lord's Supper and baptism have unique importance for the sustenance of the church. Their observance foreshadows the right subjection to God which the risen Lord will bring in the eschaton. The Supper proclaims "the Lord's death until he comes" to consummate the kingdom (1 Cor. 11:26). It forces attention on the eschatological significance of the ministry of the kingdom that led to Jesus' death: it is an eschatological meal. Its performance challenges the pretensions of the perverted powers by proclaiming this world as awaiting its redemption when the Lord returns. Thus, it reminds us that human strivings will not save the world. Only God's eschatological action will fulfill the kingdom.

Observing the Lord's Supper reminds us also that rebellious political structures killed the Lord, and that his followers are to imitate his ministry in ways that may well lead to their deaths (Matt. 10:38).[33] The Supper displays the brokenness of a world that rejected the Lord who offers himself for its salvation. In contrast to the factions of the world, the unity of believers is also proclaimed in the Supper. "Because there is one bread, we who are many are one body, for we all partake of the one bread" (1 Cor. 10:17). This unity, also proclaimed in baptism, stands in diametrical opposition to the discriminations, prejudices, and power structures of a fallen culture, as well as of a culturally accommodated church.

> As many of you as were baptized into Christ have clothed yourselves with Christ. There is no longer Jew or Greek . . . slave or free . . . male or female; for you are all one in Christ Jesus (Gal. 3:27-28).

The act of baptism, which manifests death to sin, describes this world and its rebellion against God as sinful, a realm to be judged and found wanting. It is a practice which challenges the claims of the powers of this world to be beyond corruption by proclaiming that people must die and be raised up with Christ in order to live rightly (Rom. 6:4-14). By this critical function, it calls for the praxis of faithfulness to the risen Lord in the context of the kingdom.

The observance of baptism demands that Christians walk in newness of life and pursue a lifestyle that manifests the service of God in a sinful world. In this way, the moral formation of the Christian commences at the beginning of the Christian life, symbolized by baptism. Its practice demands present obedience to God of the sort that will be fulfilled in the eschaton. Baptism marks or identifies the Christian as part of the embodied faithfulness to God that the church is to be. It calls the Christian to proper discipleship.

James McClendon in *Ethics: Systematic Theology* makes the point that "baptism points to, refers to, the life-story of Jesus himself." Disciples take up Jesus' fidelity to the kingdom by participating in this practice of incorporation into kingdom ministry. Baptism also "focuses the candidate's own life-story" as one of faithfulness to God. It brings the narratives of Jesus and the believer "into connection with one another in the company of all the saints."

In this way, it is "a narrative identification" with Jesus as "the incarnate, obedient, crucified and risen one." McClendon asks, "What, then, can the life of the baptized community be but a sharing in the eschatological freedom of the risen Lord?" The baptized people form a body without social distinctions (Gal. 3:27-29; 1 Cor. 12:12-31; Col. 3:9-11). That body is to manifest proper social relations for

> a new era in time, inaugurated by Jesus' resurrection, in which the ordinary distinctions of creation (male-female) and of society (Greek-Jew; slave-free) were superseded because unity in the body of Christ took their place.[34]

The Lord's Supper and baptism are central practices of the church also because it is through them that Christians identify themselves and their communities with primary reference and relationship to Jesus Christ. In entering the church through baptism, we are identified with the crucified and risen Lord (Rom. 6:4-11). In partaking of the Lord's Supper, we remember Jesus' ministry and death and proclaim his return by consuming "my body" and "my blood" (1 Cor. 11:24-26). These practices identify the church and the Christian as entities which see life, death, resurrection, and the future in light of the past and future of the Christ.

This same Lord demanded that his followers "seek first" God's kingdom, that they subordinate all other identities and responsibilities to those demanded by him (Matt. 6:33; Luke 9:59-62). Such is the stringent quality of faithfulness to which the church is called, through the Supper and baptism, to manifest in its common life.

The mere performance of the practices of the Lord's Supper

and baptism cannot, however, guarantee that the church will manifest a proper communal discipleship. Their performance may be, and often has been, undertaken in a fashion that neither identifies nor challenges the corrupt powers of the world.

Paul, for example, warns against improper participation in the Supper in 1 Corinthians 11:27-34. The phenomenon of people who are baptized and partake of the Lord's Supper, and yet continue boldly in sin, demonstrates that there is no automatic relationship between participation and moral formation. Some people who participate in the practices of the church do not grow as disciples. That is an indication, among other things, of the church falling short of manifesting socially a foretaste of God's reign.

Such failure shows the ambiguity of ecclesial life between the times. The church never perfectly embodies faithfulness to God, as Augustine notes in *The City of God:*

> So, too, as long as she is a stranger in the world, the city of God has in her communion, and bound to her by the sacraments, some who shall not eternally dwell in the lot of the saints. Of these, some are not now recognized; others declare themselves, and do not hesitate to make common cause with our enemies in murmuring against God, whose sacramental badge they wear. These men [and women] you may today see thronging the churches with us, tomorrow crowding the theaters with the godless. . . . These two cities are entangled together in this world, and intermixed until the last judgment effects their separation.[35]

Following the comments of Paul and of Augustine, we must have a sober recognition that the church, at least this side of the eschaton, inevitably fails to manifest unambiguously a foretaste of God's reign. Even with this realism about the church in mind, it is still appropriate to think of the Lord's Supper and baptism as central practices of the church which identify the world and the church as between Pentecost and Parousia.

The Lord's Supper and baptism are practices that call for the contextualization and critique of the everyday habits and power structures which order human life in sinful ways, even in the church. These rituals are enacted proclamations to guide the creation and sustenance of communities that embody the new age begun in Jesus' resurrection. The sustenance of their vigilance against sinful structures requires their performance in the midst of a community that under the Spirit's guidance is becoming an embodiment of true discipleship.

Since this eschatologically located task of sustaining the church is not simply a theoretical exercise, it is crucial to examine the social conditions within which the production of such a community may occur. In *Religion and Social Theory: A Materialist Perspective*, Bryan Turner makes an important argument on the role of religion within late capitalist society. Though Turner is not a theologian, his analysis highlights the importance of sustaining social structures for Christian formation. He thinks that Western society

> is characterized by a thick network of regulatory institutions which order and contain human activity. The compensation for containment is located in a hedonistic mass, consumerism, and privatized leisure.[36]

Now "private systems of meaning have become uncoupled from public modes of social legitimation." Hence, in pursuing a particular view of the good life,

> opting for abstinence or orgy is now an idiosyncratic choice without major social significance; both asceticism and hedonism are highly commercialized, operating outside zones of political regulation and administration.[37]

The only link between the private realm of freedom and "the objective regulation of public activities" is "a commercialized popular culture that employs sexual idioms to extend the market for consumer goods."[38]

Turner insists that, due to the power and structures of late capitalism, Christianity is irrelevant for the functioning of contemporary social orders. Following his line of reasoning, we see that social resistance must be mounted against the dominant forces brought to bear upon Christians in matters of everyday life such as employment, education, governmental participation, media influence, and the myriad other regimentations of life in contemporary society. Unless that is done, our desires, tastes, and habits likely will be shaped primarily by those corrupting forces.[39] The habituation of a culture that is in rebellion against God will form us into people who do not manifest discipleship to the risen Lord. Without a resistant church counterculture, our everyday lives will be ordered by priorities other than the gospel.

James Cone recounts how the white church in Bearden, Arkansas, failed to be such a resistant community. It was consequently accommodated to the norms of the surrounding culture:

> To be put in one's place, as defined by white society, was a terrible reality for blacks in Bearden. It meant being beaten by the town cop and spending an inordinate length of time in a stinking jail . . . [and] refusing to retaliate when called a nigger. . . . You had no name except your first name or "boy." . . . The white people of Bearden, of course, thought of themselves as "nice" white folks. They did not lynch and rape niggers, and many attended church every Sunday. They honestly believed that they were Christian people, faithful servants of God. Their affirmation of faith in Jesus Christ was a source of puzzlement to me, because they excluded blacks not only socially but also from their church services.[40]

Only some form of alternative, critical social order that directly combats perverse cultural influences, such as racism, will be able to produce people who can maintain vigilance against the dominant order.[41]

Such vigilance is not, however, to be equated with moral perfection or total freedom from sin. It is, nevertheless, a necessary condition for Christians who wish to pursue discipleship faithfully. Our vigilance against the sinful ways of the world is always imperfect, and our faithfulness in discipleship is always compromised. In other words, we rely ultimately on God's grace for salvation, not on some self-generated righteousness. It is of a piece with that recognition, however, to suggest that the practices of the church may serve as instruments of God's grace to enable our faithfulness, to demonstrate through us that faith requires good works (James 2:14-26).

Robert E. Webber and Rodney Clapp address the description of such a resistant ecclesial order in *People of the Truth: The Power of the Worshipping Community in the Modern World*. They explain that by

> taking up the alternative identity and vision borne by its story and signified by the cross, the church becomes a community of people free from the powers and proclaims that freedom to all who see it.[42]

Through the phenomena of its social life, the church "contradicts what the world takes to be reality. . . . The ultimate objective of its contradiction is to point to Christ." By striving to be a distinct social order, the church becomes a "diacritical community . . . [which] goes one step beyond criticism and distinguishes an alternative. . . . [It represents] a distinctive, alternative identity and vision."[43]

Webber and Clapp suggest four identifying characteristics of the diacritical community. First, such an order will be distinguished by "giftedness." The Spirit's gifts function "to integrate and strengthen the body." For the judging of gifts, they follow "Paul's criterion of solidarity: the goodness and appropriateness of an ability or gift is judged by whether or not it builds up the body."[44] Second, they distinguish the church as an "eschatological community," in which by the power of the Spirit the "peace of God's kingdom begins. In this sense the church is the beginning of the future of the world."[45] Third, it is also a community of forgiveness where God's forgiveness is the basis for a social life of reconciliation, in keeping with Paul's charge to

> bear with one another and, if anyone has a complaint against another, forgive each other; just as the Lord has forgiven you, so you also must forgive (Col. 3:13).[46]

Their fourth and most interesting characteristic of the church is "community of presence." They teach that the social reality of the church must make "God real by telling the world the story of God's intervention on its behalf and by embodying God's love and justice in the world."[47] Webber and Clapp thus call for the

church to be "the demonstration of the possibility of a new vision and a new identity, a surprising and creative cruciform vision and identity."[48]

Building on the previous analysis of Yoder, Foucault, Berkhof,
and Turner, the discussion of Webber and Clapp intensifies our
awareness of the need for a more precise account of the production of such a community of presence. In other words, it forces
the questions: What precisely must the church do and be for it
to manifest a social order that challenges the dominant order in
light of the reign of God begun in Jesus' resurrection? How does
it become a gifted, reconciled, and present community as a foretaste of the kingdom?

Guidance for the Church at Corinth

To respond to these questions, let us study Paul's advice in
1 Corinthians on aspects of ecclesial order and practice necessary for a common life in keeping with the demands of God's
reign. Early in the letter, Paul regrets that he can not address his
readers as spiritual people, but as people of flesh, "infants in
Christ" (1 Cor. 3:1). They have failed in grasping the implications of God's wisdom. They are still operating by the wisdom of
the world, not under the eschatological guidance of the Spirit.
They are "still of the flesh, . . . behaving according to human
inclinations" (3:3), not as a temple of the Holy Spirit (3:16).

Against such characteristics, Paul rejects the idea that the
Christian life is simply a matter of human striving, as "neither
the one who plants nor the one who waters is anything, but only
God who gives the growth" (3:7). The "foundation" of the Christian life is Jesus Christ, who as God's wisdom is foolishness in
"this age" (3:11, 18-19). At the same time, Paul urges his readers
to "be imitators of me" and sends Timothy as an example to remind them "of my ways in Christ" (4:16-17).

Paul treats a case of sexual immorality by insisting that such
behavior should not be tolerated in the community of faith (5:1-
2). Since the Corinthians actually boasted of this spectacle, it is
clear that they live according to the wisdom of the world, the
dominant social order of rebellion, and not as a foretaste of the
new age. Paul calls for the expulsion of the offending member as

the removal of "the yeast of malice and evil," in order that the community might become "a new batch" of "the unleavened bread of sincerity and truth" (5:7-8). The expulsion of the offender is both the removal of the one who stood in the way of their Spirit-directed life and an attempt to help him toward final salvation (5:5).

Paul notes that the Holy Spirit gives diverse spiritual gifts for the common good of the church. God distributes the gifts according to the Lord's design (12:4-11). Similarly, the one body of Christ has many members: God calls Christians with particular gifts to diverse tasks for the good of the body (12:12-31). God orders the gifts and callings of Christians toward the maturity and strength of the congregation in God's service.

First Corinthians contains numerous references to Christian growth. Paul refers to "the mature" (2:6), "infants in Christ" (3:1), the "weak" Christians (8:10-11), and his own self-discipline for spiritual formation (9:27; 13:11). He holds himself up to be imitated as a model of Christian living and sends Timothy as an example to the Corinthians (4:16-17). The dispositions of faith, hope, and love represent Paul's understanding of qualities that are necessary for Christian growth, that direct spiritual gifts rightly (13:1-13). The gifts of tongues, prophecy, knowledge, and faith must be exercised in accordance with the right kind of love in order for them to be of benefit. Even extreme self-sacrifice requires the proper disposition of the Christian for it to be worthwhile (13:1-3).

Paul's concept of love requires that it be patient, kind, not jealous, humble, proper, meek, forgiving, righteous, trusting, hopeful, and enduring (13:4-7). This sort of love serves, within the context of hope for future salvation, as the central quality necessary for the practical discernment which Paul undertakes in the epistle. It is a disposition which requires other dispositions for its right exercise. Factions arise among the spiritually stunted due to "jealousy and quarreling" about misplaced loyalty to Apollos and Cephas (1:12; 3:1-9). Improper boasting demonstrates that the Corinthians are not rightly humble, in contrast to Paul's example (4:6-16).

If the Corinthians were spiritually mature, they would not tolerate sexual immorality in the congregation, both for the sake of the offender and for the health of the community (5:1-13). Litigation between Christians reveals a lack of forgiveness and trust (6:1-8). Paul calls for mutual selfless service in relations between spouses, and a believing spouse should not leave an unbelieving mate for the sake of both the unbeliever and the children (7:1-14).

The full service of God by the unmarried (7:35), the limitation of freedom for the sake of the other (8:10-11), and Paul's becoming a slave for the gospel (9:19) are all particular implications of love as the central virtue of the Christian life. Likewise, the right use of spiritual gifts demands humility, cooperation, and concern for the edification of fellow believers (12:1-31; 14:1-40).

The point is not that Paul has a love monism and makes an explicit casuistical appeal to some independent principle of love to decide every case or issue. Rather, love is a fruit of the Spirit which should permeate the entirety of Christian existence. Love is also the central virtue of the Christian life, a characteristic or disposition necessary for relating rightly to God and humanity, and for discerning what the Christian life requires. Paul exhorts that love demands patience, kindness, humility, endurance, faith, and hope (13:4-7). He individuates faith, hope, and love as abiding dispositions, but insists that love is the greatest of the three (13:13). Paul's treatment of these qualities comes in the midst of his discussion of the use of spiritual gifts (12:1—14:40). The diversity of callings should produce harmony in the body of Christ (12:22-31). Then Paul comes to the explicit statement on love (13:1-13) and follows that statement with an argument for the superiority of prophecy over speaking in tongues (14:1-25).

The location of this passage demonstrates that Paul's interest in faith, hope, and love is not purely speculative. Indeed, he analyzes those virtues simply because they help him respond to the Corinthian situation. The Corinthians would be able to live as a proleptic social embodiment of the kingdom if they would embody the disposition of love as Paul describes it. Patience, kindness, humility, propriety, and trust would calm their arguments and provide peaceable attitudes for the resolution of many disputes. Paul makes no definite reference to love in treating some Corinthian problems, such as the litigation question (6:1-8). Yet in every problem he handles, the qualities attributed to love are embodied in his solution.

It is important to remember Arrington's account of the eschatological significance for Paul of the presence of the Holy Spirit as the inbreaking of the kingdom.[49] Diverse spiritual gifts are manifestations of that presence for the strengthening of the church as a foretaste of the new age begun in Jesus' resurrection. The Spirit enables a communal imitation of Jesus through prophecy, teaching, and other gifts. Faith, hope, and love are qualities necessary for the right use of those gifts between Pentecost and Parousia; they are dispositions required for the kingdom's journey.

Love must be the central virtue because Christian faith is grounded in the claim that "God proves his love for us in that while we still were sinners Christ died for us" (Rom. 5:8). Paul's argument is of a piece with 1 John 4:11: "Since God loved us so much, we also ought to love one another." Having love toward one's fellow Christians is part of imitating Christ.

We must remember, however, that love is an eschatologically located virtue: the location between Pentecost and Parousia defines it and makes it necessary for the Christian life. First Corinthians 13 appears in the middle of a discourse on spiritual gifts. In the community those gifts are manifestations of the inbreaking of the kingdom, the messianic presence of God. Love becomes a virtue necessary for using those gifts rightly until they cease with the Parousia (13:8). Through relationship to God and others, Christians become able to manifest the new age in their common life. Faith and hope are similarly located; they have specific reference to the Lord who will return.

In 1 Corinthians Paul does not articulate an explicit moral psychology. To discern how the dispositions of faith, hope, and love work for him, it is imperative to observe his practical, communal treatment of the Christian life. Crucial for Paul is the pursuit of the "unhindered devotion to the Lord" (7:35) that makes him "a slave to all" for the sake of the gospel (9:19). In order to help the Corinthians become imitators of such selfless devotion, he insists that they live according to the wisdom of God (3:18-23), shun members who persist in immorality (5:11), and use spiritual gifts for mutual edification (14:1-40).

For Paul, the church, revealed as a foretaste of the kingdom through spiritual gifts, needs to exhibit the kind of love that will nurture and guide members in the right imitation of Christ. Examples, imitation, and discipline have a role in the Christian life only within the context of God's grace in Jesus Christ. Between Pentecost and Parousia, Christians must have faith, hope, and love rightly if they are to become spiritually mature in subjection to God (13:9-13). Faith, hope, and love function for Paul as qualities necessary for the right use of spiritual gifts in sustaining the church as a foretaste of the new age, as the social manifestation of the inbreaking kingdom.

As seen above, Paul gives an explicitly eschatological treatment of dispositions necessary for Christian growth and for the faithfulness of the church until the Parousia. Thus he provides resources for describing the social production of discipleship as the journey of following Jesus of Nazareth in the faith community that proleptically embodies the new age. This is the case because discipleship by its very nature is the communally located task of becoming a foretaste of the end through right faithfulness to God. The object of discipleship is the Lord who has begun the end of history. Within this context it is appropriate to speak of qualities or practices that discipleship entails, or to speak of an exemplary or a poor disciple. In order to do this with precision, some account must be provided of what dispositions, traits, or structures are important for sustaining and guiding the pursuit of discipleship.

An important task of Christian ethics is to display what sort of life discipleship requires. Toward that end, we may identify virtues as enduring dispositions attributable to a self that disciples need if they are to follow the Lord rightly. There are two important checks on this task: (1) The development of virtues is not to be construed as works righteousness apart from God's grace. (2) The virtues are to be construed in a community-dependent fashion, such that the church remains the social locus of the Christian life.

The first check insists that it is only on the basis of God's gracious love that Jesus calls us to follow him and the Spirit empowers and guides us in the paths of righteousness. The second check points to the location of the Christian within a community which proleptically embodies the kingdom through the power of the Spirit, thereby challenging individualistic accounts of the Christian life.

From 1 Corinthians 13, we may identify faith, hope, and love as important individuations for thinking about the qualities that mature disciples need. Romans 12, James 2, 1 John 3, and numerous other biblical passages record instruction or examples from which other virtues may be gleaned for the Christian life. Our goal is not to provide an abstract account of how those particular virtues might be worked out. Instead, it will suffice to suggest that the church may individuate any number of virtues or identify any number of communal forces which it finds necessary for its sustenance as a foretaste of the kingdom. This process may occur as the faith community learns to embody what the central practices of baptism and the Lord's Supper display.

Informed by its embodied experience, the church may identify qualities and practices necessary for those who seek to be disciples of the risen and returning Lord. Particular understandings of virtues will be tested by whether they prove helpful for facilitating the task of discipleship. This practical, communal emphasis thus points to resources sufficient to sustain the development of the gifts of the Spirit throughout the many facets of ecclesial life.

The church strives to embody the new age in various situations through its right use of spiritual gifts expressed through individual believers "for the common good" (1 Cor. 12:7). It may emphasize helpfulness, boldness, patience, meekness, and other spiritual qualities as virtues that must characterize the lives of all its members.[50] There is some circularity between the possession of these qualities by particular Christians and the communal embodiment of them: a faithful community forms faithful people who form the community. That we may attribute such qualities to both communities and particular people (e.g., a loving church or a loving Christian), reflects a continuity of identity for the group and the self such that both entities remain accountable for deviations from that identity.

Because people undertake discipleship uniquely within the Christian community, the qualities necessary for the Christian life cannot be discerned or embodied apart from the Spirit-led life of the church. As such, there is no escape from assessing qualities required of both the community and its members in the pursuit of serving God. We are held accountable by God, the Author and Finisher of all that is. Therefore, we require enduring qualities which will sustain us until the Parousia, which will order us according to God's purposes despite our existence in a fallen world. The community of discipleship plays a unique role in fostering these virtues in the lives of its members.

Such dispositions may be attributed to both individual Christians and the church because each has an identity over time which requires faithfulness to God. I am called to be a certain kind of human being, and my congregation is called to be a certain kind of social group. Thus both my church and I must have qualities in the fashion appropriate to a particular Christian or congregation. I learn to be a disciple uniquely within a faith community, and I play a part in shaping its ethos, so the process is circular. The identification of the qualities that I or my church requires should be carried out along the path of discipleship, in the midst of our praxis. Hence, matters of virtue cannot be separated from matters of ecclesiology. The *I* cannot be separated from the *we*.

This emphasis on the communal location of the Christian life builds on the earlier discussion of Yoder. It demonstrates that questions of the identity and practice of the church as an eschatological community are profoundly important for the description of ethics. Indeed, discipleship is an intelligible notion only within the context of the social location of "the body of Christ" that lives as a foretaste of the new age through the power of the Spirit (1 Cor. 12:27).

Apart from such a community, there exist no socially embodied practices, procedures, and structures to sustain the following of Jesus. Outside the church, discipleship is at most a notion or

theory, not an observable praxis to be pursued. Hence, its substance as the active following of Jesus is compromised: it becomes an uninteresting piece of impotent pious language with
no social concretization or relevance.

Moreover, it is helpful to remember that individualistic accounts of salvation or of the Christian life are in tension with the
eschatological thrust of Christian hope. God's coming reign of
the redemption of all reality displays the glory of God with sub-
stantially greater emphasis than the glory of any particular redeemed human being. God establishes the kingdom in Jesus, begins the new age in his resurrection, creates the church through
the Spirit, and is to consummate history in the Parousia. Here is
a salvation history in which human existence is radically contextualized by the character of God. This contextualization locates
proper faithfulness uniquely within the church. Thus Christian
ethics must focus on God's chosen communal locus of salvation
as the proleptic locus of the new age. Such a claim means that
the pursuit of the Christian life is to be discussed only within the
larger, shaping context of ecclesiology.

Hence, it is fitting to study 1 Corinthians 14 and follow Paul in
measuring matters of practical reason by how they build up the
church. That edification amounts to the task of sustaining the
church as a foretaste of the new age through the ordering of
forces, structures, and dispositions in the community in line with
the goal of a communal imitation or discipleship of Christ.
Thereby, matters as diverse as the use of spiritual gifts, litigation
between Christians, and excommunication are held in scrutiny
by the goal of manifesting faithfulness to the risen Lord. Virtually any aspect of the life of the community or of a member of the
community may become an important matter for discernment.

The Christian life, then, requires the establishment of communal forces of faithfulness to God through practices of discipleship which will sustain the church as a socially embodied
foretaste of the new age. The Christian, apart from the communal locus in which discipleship is pursued under the guidance of
the Spirit, will be overcome by the rebellious forces and powers
of this world which amount to instruments of corruption. In order to resist these forces, we need to give critical attention to

matters of everyday life that tend to shape us in keeping with the dominant ethos and subvert our lives from the faithful service of God. The church is to be a social space in which faithfulness to God is possible, from which a foretaste of the kingdom may come. Such a social space is required for Christian growth because of the rebellion of the world, the present brokenness of the human service of God.

It is crucial to remember, however, that this brokenness reaches even into the community of faith: it is not limited to the world. The church has never been morally perfect and never will be perfect before the final consummation of God's rule. All too often, Christian communities of faith seem to be molded decisively by corrupting cultural forces. Sometimes they manifest anything but a foretaste of God's new age.

The particulars of the corruption of the church will vary according to the many variables which impinge upon a given group of Christians at a given time and in a given place. Sober recognition of the temptations, perversions, and failures of the church in any historical circumstance should not, however, lead us to despair over the relevance of an approach to the Christian life which emphasizes the church's role in the moral formation of Christians.

We must remember that Paul's discourses on spiritual gifts as well as his description of faith, hope, and love, were directed toward an obviously imperfect and compromised Corinthian community of faith. Paul's language is notably *prescriptive* in tone, calling Christians to live in a manner appropriate to the demands of the gospel. He gave advice on how to respond to instances of gross sexual immorality and strife among fellow members so severe that they were seeking justice in pagan courts (5:1—6:8). Thus Paul was grappling with real-life issues of congregational practice, not with lofty abstractions of moral theory.

Our discussion of communal moral formation has a strong reliance upon practices of the church which resist the corrupting forces of the world. It is likewise a prescriptive account of how the church might go about responding to the plethora of moral ambiguities which it faces. We may respond to ecclesiastical shortcomings with practices, structures, and procedures which impinge directly upon particular temptations that are pressing in a given instance. Thereby the community of faith will find resources, under the guidance of the Spirit, for resisting corruptions of the world and manifesting a foretaste of God's reign in its common life.

One congregation, for example, might need to find ways of including or identifying with Christians of other races in order to combat racism in the community of faith. Another might need to find ways of affirming the equality of women in the church, of challenging an idolatrous patriotism, or of combating cultural notions about economics which may preclude Christians from the proper use of wealth. Depending upon the dynamics of their particular situations, most congregations would benefit from prayerful attempts to address obstacles to faithfulness in such explicit, embodied ways.

In our approach we do not assume, then, that every social grouping or institution which calls itself church is a shining bastion of faithfulness to the gospel. We do not imagine that there exists anywhere on earth a group of Christians whose common life is free from sin of any kind. Our discussion of the church has not been *descriptive* in this sense. Instead, the crucial point is that any group which claims to be church should be held accountable to what the church ought to be. An eschatological view of the church as a foretaste of the new age provides substantial conceptual resources for calling any group of Christians to greater fidelity to the gospel. It displays the profound moral seriousness of undertaking to be the church. By accepting that task, a community finds itself responsible to meet the challenge of embodying proleptically God's reign.

In discussing how we may resist the failures and corruptions of the church, it is important to keep foremost in mind that we live in a period of time in which God's reign has begun but has not yet been consummated. Jesus' ministry and resurrection, the coming of the Spirit at Pentecost, and the faithful life of the church are all signs of the kingdom's inbreaking. Yet strong indications remain in human history of the persistence of the world's rebellion against God. We notice threats of nuclear war, environmental destruction, varieties of social inequality, and the often uncritical "baptism" of dominant cultural forces by Christians. These are but a few indications that we live *between* the times, not in the time of the kingdom's unambiguous fulfillment.

Awareness of this historical ambiguity and tension demands a restless vigilance on the part of the church against worldly corruption and unwarranted cultural accommodation. Regardless of how faithful we perceive ourselves to be, we may be sure that *we have not yet arrived.* In most congregations and other denominational institutions, one does not have to look far to find substantial room for improvement in faithfulness. It is, therefore, continually fitting to examine ourselves and our churches in order to identify and resist aspects of our lives which seem to be signs of the old age of sin (Gal. 1:4), rather than of the new age of salvation, the new creation (2 Cor. 5:17). Such is the difficult struggle of groups of people who seek to embody a foretaste of a kingdom which has not yet come in its fullness.

Indeed, if we ignore the fact that the completion of salvation is a future reality, we jeopardize discipleship and communal faithfulness. Ernst Käsemann displays this fact in his claim about the situation addressed by Paul in Corinth: the root of their immorality was

> a sacramental realism which sees complete redemption to have already been effected, in that by baptism a heavenly spiritual body has been conferred and the earthly body has been degraded to an insubstantial, transitory veil.[51]

Their supposed "angelic status" gave license to ways of behavior that did not reflect the service of God. Indeed, for Paul "Christ's mission and presence was not, and is not, first and foremost to individuals" whose salvation endows them with freedom from the responsibilities of bodily action.[52] On the contrary, hope in the future of the risen Lord locates individual Christians within the church as the unique locus of discipleship. Believers may learn to be rightly obedient to God in the midst of a rebellious world only by taking up the difficult journey of the kingdom under the guidance of the Spirit in the community of faith. The eschatological location requires struggle in the present against perverted powers that may be resisted uniquely by the socially embodied witness of the church as a foretaste of the kingdom.

In fact, the moral life of the Christian finds intelligibility only within a community which embodies socially the discipleship of Jesus. Since Christian ethics has the primary task of sustaining the embodied process of pursuing faithfulness in community, the moral identity of the individual Christian is radically contextualized by that social location. Paul's argument in 1 Corinthians 12—14 that spiritual gifts be exercised in accord with the edification of the community is a good example of how the role of the particular Christian should be seen within the larger shaping context of the church.

Notice a further implication of this approach to understanding the Christian life: it is a serious theological mistake to construe the identity of the Christian as a moral agent apart from primary reference to the life of the community. To do so would be analogous to speaking of the integrity of a part of a body without reference to the other parts and their common function. A hand, apart from its status as a member of a human body, has no intelligibility as a hand. Likewise, discipleship has no intelligibility apart from its display in and through the social order called church. Unless there are practices and structures in the church to form and support the believer, the Christian life becomes dubious. The lone Christian, disconnected from the support of the practices of the community, will find it exceedingly difficult to pursue discipleship well.

Because our salvation is not yet fulfilled, discipleship requires a social locus of resistance to present corruption. The ethic of the new age calls for the embodied process of discipleship which marks a group of people as church in the midst of a rebellious world. Such a process is the concretization of hope in the future of the risen Lord: it makes sense only in light of the future created by Jesus' resurrection. It requires the manifestation of the praxis of faithfulness to the Lord who will return to work history's full subordination to God. That future locates our present and identifies the church as the embodied social reality which has the difficult tasks of discerning and displaying the practices of discipleship in a world which has not yet become subordinate to God's rule.

Moral Description and Practical Reason in Eschatological Context

The church should exercise moral discernment as a foretaste of the new age and enable its members to pursue discipleship faithfully. That discernment is decisively shaped and informed by the eschatological expectation created by Jesus' resurrection. We can see how eschatology influences such discernment by examining the relevance of eschatology for moral descriptions and practical rationality.

Moral descriptions or definitions of moral terms, such as *justice*, are crucial for understanding materially how a moral project will proceed and what ends it will pursue. It is only through using practical reason, actual moral judgment on particular matters, that descriptive terms will be produced, employed in statements, and applied in given situations.

These claims are justified because moral qualifiers are terms that provide a way of describing the ethical significance of a particular event, situation, or person.[1] For example, we may speak of a just cause, a just situation, or a just person when we wish to describe these entities as characterized by justice. How the content of terms of moral description will be formulated is a crucial

matter for any moral project. The meaning of the moral statement depends on the definition of the qualifying term.

For example, when justice is understood as a function of respect for property rights, the claim "Jones is a just human being"
will indicate that the speaker thinks that Jones is characterized
by proper respect for such rights. On the other hand, when the
pursuit of social equality is made constitutive of the definition of
justice, the claim that "Jones is a just human being" will indicate
that the speaker thinks that Jones is characterized by the pursuit
of social equality, that Jones orders other concerns, such as respect for property rights, in accord with the goal of equality.[2]

The meaning of a moral statement hinges on the definition of
the operative descriptive term (e.g., *justice*). We therefore must
examine how terms of moral description are produced, defined,
and applied in a proper eschatological and communal context.
Since this volume is an exercise in Christian ethics, our discussion must provide an account of how the theological modifier,
and especially the temporal eschatological context, materially
shape the standards, terms, and procedures of ethical judgment
and analysis within the pursuit of discipleship. This judgment
will focus on matters encountered in the course of human living.
Hence, it is fundamentally a practical endeavor of describing,
evaluating, and discerning among the particulars of life.

Theological Grounds for a Narrative Description

Our first task in constructing such an account is to display why
the theological notions addressed in previous chapters lead naturally to, and may have relevance for, a discussion of descriptive
moral analysis. Here it is important to note the basic Christian
belief that the risen Lord is the agent of both the creation and final redemption of the universe. This belief provides solid theological grounds for insisting that all reality, and surely forms of
discourse such as ethics, be construed in light of the character of
the God known in Jesus (John 1:3; Col. 1:15-16). As this God is
Alpha and Omega (Rev. 1:8), we must discern the significance
of human behavior in a manner appropriate to the location of
the behavior within God's universe.

Because we recognize the claim God has on us by virtue of

our status as parts of creation, Christians are justified in thinking that proper human behavior and existence should display discipleship: the active following of the Lord in and through the practices of the community which seeks to embody proleptically the redemption of the world. The risen Lord is the key to the destiny of all reality, including humankind. Hence, Christians should discern the significance of human behavior and carry out the task of moral description in willing subjection to God and anticipation of the future subjection of all things to God (1 Cor. 15:24-28). In this sense, we must learn to describe morality in light of what we confess as true and what we expect on the basis of Jesus' resurrection. But how do we gain conceptual clarity on the nature of this task?

A way of getting a handle on the specifics of this endeavor is to examine Alasdair MacIntyre's position on the description of human behavior within a narrative social context. In *After Virtue* he notes how observers describe action:

> We place the agents' intentions . . . with reference to their role in the history of the setting or settings to which they belong. . . . Narrative history of a certain kind turns out to be the basic and essential genre for the characterization of human actions.[3]

MacIntyre provides an example to display how intelligible action requires location within a narrative. He asks us to imagine someone saying to him, "The name of the common wild duck is *Histrionicus histrionicus histrionicus*." In order to provide an account of what the person was doing in uttering those words, MacIntyre says that he would have to locate the statement within one of several possible narrative construals. For example, the speaker might have mistaken MacIntyre for someone who had earlier asked him the Latin name for the common wild duck, he might be saying whatever came to mind as a therapeutic exercise to overcome shyness, or he might be a spy attempting to identify himself to his contact. "In each case the act of utterance becomes intelligible by finding its place in a narrative."[4]

Not only conversation, but "all human transactions in general" have a narrative quality for MacIntyre. An important implication of his approach is that actions require a setting, a context, a location within a set of shared expectations for their intelligibility, their meaningful description. "If in the middle of my lecture on Kant's ethics I suddenly broke six eggs into a bowl and added flour and sugar, proceeding all the while with my Kantian exegesis, I have not . . . performed an intelligible action."[5]

Moral descriptions are one instance of statements about intelligible action. To say that Jones is just requires that we have made sense of Jones's actions. Hence, it is possible to use MacIntyre's analysis in a way that will illumine the moral relevance of eschatology. Namely, the Christian story about the Christ as the agent of both the creation and coming redemption of the universe provides a narrative context in light of which Christians may describe the moral significance of human action.

This expectation has a narrative form in that Christians see themselves and all reality in the midst of a sequence of events, located between Pentecost and Parousia, that has a temporal character. Believers look forward to the kingdom's consummation, which is a discrete event to occur in the future, on the basis of Jesus' resurrection. We see reality as part of this story of God's redemption.[6]

An important implication of this narrative is the claim that humans must become disciples and follow the Lord who is the key to the end of the story in the community that foreshadows that end. This is necessary if we are to live in a manner appropriate to characters in the cosmic drama through which Christians are to see reality. The centrality of this eschatological story for Christian belief becomes obvious: apart from the narrative of hope created by Jesus' resurrection, the identity of the church as a foretaste of the new age becomes unintelligible.

Outside this context of expectation, the practices of baptism, the Lord's Supper, and the entire pursuit of discipleship simply do not make sense, at least not in the way that Christians have traditionally understood them. It is hard to know, for example, what it would mean to "proclaim the Lord's death until he comes" (1 Cor. 11:26) without a temporal context which provides warrants for why and how such proclamation is important. On the other hand, tasks of discipleship become the uniquely appropriate forms of action for those who see themselves located between Pentecost and Parousia, who seek to understand reality in accord with the future of the risen Lord.

Such expectation is to shape the way Christians see themselves and the world. It should play a decisive role in how we describe the moral significance of human action, for all human action occurs in this storied world. John Howard Yoder points toward the importance of this sort of description in his essay "Armaments and Eschatology." He states that to sing the song of Revelation 5:12,

> "The Lamb Is Worthy to Receive Power,". . . is not mere poetry. It is performative proclamation. It redefines the cosmos in a way prerequisite to the moral independence which it takes to speak truth to power and to persevere when no reward is in sight.[7]

Yoder sees that this early Christian affirmation challenges "the notion that the ruler is the primary agent of divine movement in history." The risen Lord, not the sitting monarch, will be the Victor. Hence, hope in the future of this risen Lord "may free us to live without the myth of a complete systematic causal overview of how all that we do will work out for the best, because we see things whole and intervene 'responsibly.' "

Yoder's point is that humans may refrain from describing reality as destined for subjection to God in the finale or future fulfillment of the eschatological story that Christians confess. Thus humans may come under the illusion that they are in control of history. We may come to view the course of human events primarily as a realm susceptible to manipulation for our own ends, and hence we may pursue an ethic which implies humanity's ultimate sovereignty.

Consequentialist moral reasoning may be "appropriate to a setting where the agents dispose of considerable power over events and far-reaching knowledge of the pertinent causal connections." Yet Yoder argues that it is illusory for humans to entertain the possibility of the destruction of human life on earth by nuclear holocaust as though it were such a tidy conceptual matter. Against that Promethean self-deception, he proposes that a return to "the hymnic vision of a cosmos smaller than the God who made it and sent His son and us to redeem it will relativize both the gloomy and the confident determinisms to which we have been captive."

The claim that the crucified and risen Lord, not "the cult of Caesars old and new," is the key to "righteousness in the world" frees us from slavery to modern humanistic myths of despair or hubris about the outcome of history. Against commonplace assumptions about power and influence, Christians believe that "people who bear crosses are working with the grain of history."[8]

Yoder's argument highlights the descriptive relevance of the church's eschatological faith: we see reality as a realm of which God, not humanity, is the Lord. We believe that, even as God overcame the obscene death of the Messiah in Jesus' resurrection, all reality will one day be fully subject to God in the consummated kingdom. Hence, the defining events of history are the Lord's incarnation, living example, ministry, death and resurrection, sending of the Spirit at Pentecost, and future Parousia. For the Christian, these function as the most decisive events, the major narrative reference points for describing the significance of human action.

This orientation invites the self-conscious, explicit description of events as happenings in a world whose redemption, begun in Jesus' resurrection, has not yet been fulfilled. Within this temporal narrative context, discipleship is the uniquely appropriate mode of life. The Jesus whom disciples follow is the risen Lord in whose future lies the destiny of the universe. Likewise, church becomes a crucially important form of social organization for humans in God's world, as it has the task of foreshadowing the future which God will bring.

To stress the point, these statements about discipleship and church are warranted precisely by their location within a temporal eschatological context. I describe them as crucial matters due to their significance in an eschatological scheme which sees the world destined for subjection to God in the eschaton. In that such expectation is the foundation for these views of discipleship and church, it will have relevance for shaping the nature of the moral rationality appropriate to the Christian life. The rationality which produces the statements on discipleship and church is itself part of the narrative: it is moral discernment in a world destined for God's full redemption.

Practical Rationality

To begin to display the significance of the eschatological context for Christian moral rationality, it is again helpful to turn to MacIntyre. In *Whose Justice? Which Rationality?* he argues that descriptions of both moral norms and reason are dependent upon traditions which vary according to the particulars of social location and history:

> In Aristotelian practical reasoning it is the individual *qua* citizen who reasons; in Thomistic practical reasoning it is the individual *qua* inquirer into his or her own good and the good of his or her community; in Humean practical rationality it is the individual *qua* propertied or unpropertied participant in a society of a particular kind of mutuality and reciprocity; but in the practical reasoning of liberal modernity it is the individual *qua* individual who reasons.[9]

The Aristotelian undertakes practical reasoning through a "practical syllogism" that entails formed judgment on action in light of the good; the liberal simply satisfies his or her desires in a world with no clear ordering of goods.[10] MacIntyre's point is that various traditions see morality differently. Their accounts of what morality concerns and how its discernment works are formed in light of particular traditions that are not necessarily commensurate. Indeed, traditions often disagree on what it would mean to be moral or to engage in moral discernment.

Let us follow MacIntyre's lead on this point by examining how Christian eschatological claims may shape a view of practical rationality. The previous chapter demonstrated that the moral discernment of the Christian life requires an ecclesial context for its intelligibility. The aim of that context is to be a proleptic social manifestation of God's reign, to embody a communal imitation of Christ. This is to be done in the power of the Spirit and through vigilance against corruption that is sustained by the performance of practices of discipleship.

Thus a first qualifier of Christian practical rationality is that it should be a communally embodied and sustained task. It is the discernment of the community of faith, a social realm seeking to be distinct from that of the rebellious world, whose primary purpose or end is to foreshadow God's reign.

Within the ecclesial context, the agent of practical reason is the disciple who is pursuing faithfulness to the way of the risen Lord. Christians identify themselves with primary reference to Jesus through the practices of baptism and the Lord's Supper. In entering the church through baptism, we are identified with the crucified and risen Lord (Rom. 6:4-11). In partaking of the Lord's Supper, we remember Jesus' ministry and death and proclaim his return by consuming "my body" and "my blood" (1 Cor. 11:24-26).

These practices identify the Christian as someone who sees his or her destiny as part of the future of the Christ. This same Lord demands that his followers "seek first" God's reign and subordinate all other identities and responsibilities to those demanded by him (Matt. 6:33; Luke 9:59-62). Hence, the individual agent of the practical reason of following Jesus is the disciple whose identity is formed through location in the narrative scheme of identifying with and following the Lord who is the key to the future, whose raising has begun a new age.

The faith community has the job of producing disciples who pursue faithfulness to Jesus as the goal of the Christian life. This goal is, in Yoder's words, formed in light of "that recorded experience of practical moral reasoning in genuine human form that bears the name Jesus."[11] Hence, it requires a mode of moral rationality that is able to identify and reject interpretations of the Christian life that hinder proper discipleship, that obscure fidelity to Jesus.

An example of this kind of discernment is Yoder's condemnation of the just-war tradition for Christians as "a fundamentally new political ethic . . . [that] rejects the privileged place of the enemy as the test of whether one loves one's neighbor. It rejects the norm of the cross and the life of Jesus Christ as the way of dealing with conflict."[12] The rise of just-war tradition "must be described as a reversal rather than as an organic development" of Christian faith. The justification of Christian participation in war is not a logical implication of the gospel in the sense of displaying the requirements of discipleship. It contradicts the very end of the Christian life, the task of faithfulness to Jesus.[13]

I have cited Yoder on this point, not to introduce a discussion of just-war tradition, but to show how the practical reason of discipleship might work. It will seek to determine whether particular involvements or commitments provide appropriate opportunities for the pursuit of discipleship, for active faithfulness to Jesus. When, in comparison with Jesus' embodied example of kingdom ministry, an option appears as a poor mode of discipleship, it will be rejected.

The practical rationality of discipleship does not, however, operate purely in this negative mode of identifying inappropriate moral projects. It may also lead Christians to acts of faithfulness to the risen Lord. To provide an example of how such reasoning might work, let us focus briefly on Luke's account of Jesus as a Messiah whose ministry extends beyond the confines of his group of followers and the pious of Israel.

According to Luke, Jesus' inaugural sermon begins with the claim that "the Spirit of the Lord is upon me, because he has anointed me to bring good news to the poor, . . . to proclaim the year of the Lord's favor" (4:18-19). Luke describes Jesus' ministry of this favorable year as conspicuous in its blessing of outcasts from proper Jewish society, such as the demonized (4:31-41), lepers (5:12), tax collectors (5:27-32), and an unclean woman (8:43). Jesus values these outcasts no less than officials of the synagogue (8:40-56). He displays a way of life that reaches out to the unclean, unorthodox, and even those patently controlled by the forces of evil. Such people are proper objects for the ministry of God's kingdom.

Luke portrays Jesus as a Messiah who pursues a ministry of physical healing, affirmation of social and religious outcasts, promotion of righteous economic activity (12:13-34), and proclamation so threatening to the rulers of his society that they seek his death (23:1-5). He describes Jesus as requiring of his followers a praxis that is equally disruptive and dangerous (9:22-24).

By attempting to follow Jesus in this sort of kingdom ministry, disciples will ask questions of practical reason: Who are the lep-

ers, the demonized, the beggars, the outcasts of our society?
What would it mean to take up Jesus' cross in our situation? How
may we be faithful to the Lord in our present circumstances? In
pursuing such questions, believers are engaged in the practical
reason of faithfulness to the risen Lord. They seek to behave in a
manner decisively informed by the example of Jesus as a Lord
who requires obedience, as the paradigm of what faithfulness to
God entails.[14] They interpret human action and circumstances
within the temporal eschatological context of a world destined
for God's final redemption in light of Jesus' resurrection.

Yoder points to another aspect of this type of discernment.
He asserts that the church's narratively shaped identity as an eschatological community gives it the practical task of discerning
how

> to be now what the world is called to be ultimately. . . . The
> church is thus not chaplain or priest to the powers running the
> world: she is called to be a microcosm of the wider society, not
> only as an idea, but also in her function.[15]

In pursuing this goal, the church establishes "pilot programs to
meet previously unmet needs or to restore ministries that have
collapsed."

The church also manifests a "subculture" of "sacramentality"
that pursues and embodies the implications of the gospel for human interaction. For example, participation in the Lord's Supper may lead to "the sharing of bread between those who have
and those who have not." Baptism is "the basis of Christian egal-
itarianism" that overcomes social distinctions. "Binding and
loosing—i.e., deliberative morally accountable dialogue, dealing
with offense and forgiveness (and thereby dealing with moral
discernment)—may recover the connection with forgiveness
and decision-making" necessary for the church to be a foretaste
of God's kingdom.[16]

There is no tension here between speaking of the task of
Christian moral rationality as "discerning how to follow Jesus in
present circumstances" and as "discerning how the church may
embody a foretaste of God's reign." The Spirit that leads the
church, that makes its faithfulness possible, is precisely the

Spirit of the risen Lord. To put it differently, discipleship requires location within the faith community, while the community's pursuit of faithfulness may be understood as the quest for a communal imitation of Christ. Both ways of putting it demonstrate that Christian practical rationality requires location within the temporal eschatological context, and that at base the problematic is that of sustaining faithfulness to the risen Lord.

Within the context of that goal, Christians should seek to live in the world in a manner appropriate to their description of it as a realm created and to be redeemed by the God who is incarnate in Jesus of Nazareth. Hence, they will discern what actions are appropriate for disciples through a rationality which has this discriminating standard: Are the particular projects proper opportunities for behavior that manifests fidelity to the Christ? The most significant distinguishing feature of this approach, to cite Yoder, is that "the story of Jesus [functions] as paradigm" for the discernment of the Christian life, which is a communal endeavor.[17] The moral agents are disciples of Jesus, and their moral rationality is understood as the task of pursuing faithfulness to the risen Lord in a world destined for subjection to the God whose new age has already begun.

Justice

In order to display with greater clarity the relevance of this view of practical reason for the Christian life, it is important to gain a clear idea of what the moral term *justice* should mean in this eschatological construct. In this context, *justice* would mean that quality characteristic of action between people which manifests proper faithfulness to God as that is known and demonstrated in Jesus Christ.

The terms of the definition entail that the significance of human social relations should be understood in light of the basic Christian conviction that one God, who is incarnate in Jesus of Nazareth, has created and will redeem the world. Hence, there is no realm of creation or moral discourse that may operate as though Jesus were not Lord, as though location in the cosmic drama of salvation were irrelevant to the task of describing proper human relations. Indeed, here the term *justice* is simply a name for the kind of social relations demanded by the claim that Jesus is Lord. It is a shorthand way of expressing that discipleship must shape the way humans relate to one another.

The New Testament provides numerous examples of what this sort of justice, or proper human interaction in the new age, requires. For instance, it entails the humble service of washing feet (John 13) as well as the pursuit of Jesus' mission to preach good news to the poor, release the captives, and give sight to the blind (Luke 4). Justice requires the life of holy sacrifice described by Paul in Romans 12. It calls the faith community to be a social setting in which Christians do not sue one another (1 Corinthians 6) and in which we do not show favoritism on account of wealth (James 2).

To describe particular situations, events, or people as just in this sense, a speaker must be a practitioner of the moral rationality of discipleship as described above. To be able to see what forms of social action manifest proper faithfulness to Jesus, one must be about the task of discipleship and be a pursuer of justice within a faith community that embodies and sustains the skills of discerning what faithfulness entails in particular situations. This claim reflects the fact that both the rationality of discipleship and the description of moral terms find their intelligibility within a single narrative construal. Both are part of the temporal eschatological drama confessed by Christians.

Hence, discerning the path of discipleship and describing moral terms are not autonomous notions. Rather, their formulation must take place in a manner appropriate to the narrative location and to their interrelation. The description of moral rationality must be of a piece with the description of central moral notions in order for the moral life to be coherent. Put another way, in order to discern as a disciple, one must be able to describe the moral significance of various entities as a disciple. Indeed, moral descriptions are terms which carry within themselves evaluative judgments on the significance of particular situations. That evaluative judgment is precisely the work of Christian moral rationality. To know when and how to apply such a judgment requires the practical discernment of discipleship.

For example, the Christian will be able to describe a particular relationship between two people as adultery because she has learned to name it as such and to describe a social phenomenon with certain characteristics as adulterous. The description of adultery is neither arbitrary nor self-evident: it depends on a definite mode of Christian moral reason, with particular convictions about what constitutes marriage and the fidelity appropriate to it. Not all people subscribe to those convictions. To say "I describe this situation as adultery" is to perform moral discernment in a fashion that requires the proper use of a descriptive term in order for the discernment to be done well. One who invokes the moral description of adultery acts as a moral agent who is accountable to others for that identification of the situation. In the community called church, discourse on terms like adultery finds its meaning.

Thus moral judgment is held accountable to the community of faith. This is another way of displaying the necessity of the church for the sustenance of the Christian life. Description and discernment are intellectual tasks of discipleship. They require location within the unique social locus of discipleship that sustains them and seeks to embody faithfulness in the midst of a rebellious world.

Crucial aspects of that embodiment are the vigilant production of moral descriptions and the exercise of moral rationality in a way that will guide well the pursuit of discipleship. These endeavors will highlight what is at stake for Christians in the circumstances which they encounter. Indeed, these tasks are nothing less than necessary strategies for seeing and living in a world destined for God's redemption.

A way of elucidating the import of this eschatologically informed view of moral description and practical rationality is to contrast it with Reinhold Niebuhr's description of justice. Niebuhr finds the commandment for sacrificial, forgiving love to be at the heart of Jesus' teaching: "The height of love is certainly more unprudential and uncalculating than mutual love and it contains universalistic demands which challenge any particular community."[18] However, love finds its source in "purely religious and not in socio-moral terms." It is essentially concerned with the individual's relationship with God, not with other people. "It has only a vertical dimension between the loving will of God and the will of man [and woman]."[19]

Niebuhr thinks that this standard of love can never be embodied or manifest in actual life; it presupposes a sinless, non-estranged moral agent. The law of love is not, then, an obligation for the Christian: it is a paradox, a goal with which compliance is impossible under the estranged conditions of historical existence.[20] Within this context, Niebuhr takes justice as an approximation of love which allows Christians to seek a balance of power in society: "The very essence of politics is the achievement of justice through equilibria of power."[21]

Duane K. Friesen in *Christian Peacemaking and International Conflict* makes the point that Niebuhr's view is

> a serious distortion of the Christian faith because it does not sufficiently emphasize the basic thrust of the whole biblical story: God's redemptive activity in history to make his people into a new people who, because of their trust in God, are given new possibilities of obedience to God's will.[22]

Niebuhr, says Friesen, makes the mistake of construing theology as a discourse primarily about "human possibility" in a fashion that makes sin inevitable and faithfulness to Jesus impossible.[23]

Friesen's claim on the centrality of anthropology for Niebuhr is borne out by his eschatology. Niebuhr's eschatology is formulated primarily in terms of a "dialectical conception of time and eternity" in which the human as a finite creature with an infinite horizon is inevitably caught.[24] Niebuhr moves from a perceptive analysis of human self-consciousness to claims about history that provide a context for the inevitably estranged human.[25] God's kingdom functions for him as an ideal, atemporal realm above human history. The kingdom symbolizes our estrangement, for we always fall short by its standard of love. The approximation of justice is, consequently, the best that we can do.

In Niebuhr's view, then, the kingdom is a transcendent symbol of sacrificial love and reminds us of the estrangement and finitude of human existence. This perspective appears to be a decisive factor in his description of justice as an approximation of love. The content of that love is not determinately informed by the discipleship of Jesus. In other words, Niebuhr's eschatological commitments are of a piece with his descriptions of Christian moral rationality and justice.

Niebuhr arrives at these conclusions because he largely collapses Christian expectation for the future coming of the kingdom into a symbol of the inevitable alienation of human existence. For Niebuhr, we are hardly located within a narrative or temporal scheme, the end of which will be the fulfillment of redemption. Instead, we are caught in a static dialectic between time and eternity. Niebuhr put it this way:

> Placing the final fulfillment at the end of time and not in a realm above temporality is to remain true to the genius of prophetic religion and to state mythically what cannot be stated rationally. If stated rationally the world is divided between the temporal and the eternal and only the eternal forms above the flux of temporality have significance. . . . The apocalypse is a mythical expression of the impossible possibility under which all human life stands . . . the Kingdom of God is therefore not here. It is in fact always coming but never here.[26]

Likewise, salvation for Niebuhr refers to human acceptance of the dialectic, not to the coming fullness of God's reign.[27] In this sense, his theology obscures the temporal hope which Christians should have on the basis of Jesus' resurrection.

In a manner consistent with his lack of a futuristic eschatology, Niebuhr did not view the church as a foretaste of the new age or the necessary social locus of the Christian life. His audience was the United States of America, and much of his work focused on advising its government and other powerful institutions on how to pursue justice. The content of the justice for which Niebuhr called was neither uniquely nor explicitly Christian, as his popularity and profound influence in non-Christian sectors demonstrated.

Dennis P. McCann claims in *Christian Realism and Liberation Theology* that Niebuhr had primarily "an ethic for politicians." He called for the achievement of balances of power as the best strategy for precluding injustice. While the idea of a balance of power reflects an insightful reading of the necessity of regulating the distribution of power in society, McCann states that Niebuhr's formulation provides

> no guidance for solving the conflict. . . . It lacks specific criteria for distinguishing the abuse of such power from its proper exercise. Niebuhr's middle axioms, in other words, remain intuitive precisely where they should be more explicit.[28]

Niebuhr would describe justice, then, as something like that quality manifest in social situations characterized by a balance of power in society.[29] Jesus functions systematically in this definition as the preacher and example of an impossible ideal of sacrificial love. That love stands above the approximation of justice, holding its historical manifestation in creative tension with an eternal ideal. Practical reason is for Niebuhr the discernment of how to "coerce the anarchy of conflicting human interests into some kind of order," to pursue justice in an inevitably sinful world. It is the intuitive task of achieving balances of power.[30]

There is also a central eschatological reason for the discrepancy between the view of moral reason which our discussion has developed and that of Niebuhr. We have seen that Jesus' resurrection inaugurates a new age of salvation that will consummate a future which is to fulfill history. Because of that, Christians are to intend themselves as disciples of the risen Lord in the community that uniquely foreshadows the kingdom through the power of the Spirit. Christian ethics, then, becomes the task of discerning what discipleship entails in particular situations through the communally sustained practical reason and moral description of the Christian life. In other words, the whole of the moral life is located explicitly in the eschatological narrative of hope in the future of the risen Lord, the narrative that places the Christian between Pentecost and Parousia.

Niebuhr, on the other hand, views the Christian life as the task of learning to accept our inevitable estrangement from the eternal, static ideals of love and the kingdom, and to pursue balances of power throughout society. There is nothing really distinctive in the Christian life in this endeavor; it is simply one form of the estranged existence that all people experience. Indeed, the *temporal future* created by Jesus' resurrection is not operative in Niebuhr's view of Christian ethics. It does not locate us or serve to describe reality within a narrative of hope for the coming kingdom. Hence, Niebuhr presents the practical reason of learning to live with alienation, to pursue a justice not directly associated with Jesus because his ethic is not suited to social relations in a sinful world.

To stress the point, discipleship is not an interesting moral notion for Niebuhr because it would imply fidelity to an ethic unsuited to the inevitability of sin. Instead, he advocates an ethic accommodated to the estranged realities of life, with balance-of-power justice as the operative moral principle.

Let us elaborate our disagreement with Niebuhr. He describes the moral realities of life primarily in terms of anthropology, not in terms of the future created by Jesus' resurrection. His determining description of our existence is that individual humans are inevitably estranged from the kingdom's ideal of love. Given that commitment, it might well follow that the task of Christian ethics is to derive some principle, such as justice, more suited to the political demands of approximating the good life in the midst of a fallen world.

However, our determining description is that Jesus has been raised from the dead and has thereby begun a sequence of resurrection in a new age of salvation that will culminate in the fullness of God's reign. For those who see themselves located within this narrative, the moral life must be one of pursuing faithfulness to the risen Lord. In our eschatological account, it is not adequate to describe Jesus as the preacher of an impossible ethic which stands above history or is essentially nontemporal.

On the contrary, Jesus is the risen and returning Lord, the agent of creation and redemption, in whose world we live, under whose dominion we are, and in whose future lies our destiny. Hence, moral terms such as justice and the task of practical reason must be described in accord with a narratively construed reality. The determining category is the promise of the risen Lord, not our sin.

This discussion of moral description in Christian ethics is not, however, of a purely abstract or metaethical relevance. How one views justice or the nature of the Christian life will have a direct

impact on casuistry, the task of making particular moral judgments in real-life situations.

For example, Yoder sees Jesus' acceptance of death on the
cross as a paradigm for the kind of nonresistant suffering that
discipleship entails. In a world over which the slain Lamb has
conquered, Christians are to accept the trials entailed by following a Lord who pursued "a moral clash with the powers ruling
his society" in such a deliberate, provocative way that his execu-
tion was virtually assured.[31] Jesus nonviolently went about the
service of God's kingdom; just so are his followers to renounce
violence as an inappropriate strategy for faithfulness to the God
whose power is manifest in the weakness of the cross.[32]

Yoder therefore refuses to understand justice in a way which
underwrites the use of violence by Christians. "That there can
be a just war in the Christian sense of the word *just* or *righteous*
is, of course, excluded by definition. . . ."[33] Justice is a characteristic of those who follow rightly a Lord who demands non-
violence. Thus, the term *justice* may not be used to describe action which is inconsistent with discipleship. In this way, Yoder
rules out the possibility that the use of violence by Christians
could be described as just.

Niebuhr reaches a different conclusion, largely because he
thinks that justice requires the exercise of political responsibility as an approximation of Jesus' impossible and atemporal ideal
of love. That approximation, however, does not embody the
nonviolent following of Jesus emphasized by Yoder. Indeed, Jesus' rejection of violent means for his kingdom ministry does not
explicitly shape Niebuhr's description of justice or his view of its
implications for the exercise of responsibility in society. Instead,
Niebuhr explains that the task of justice is the pursuit of a balance of power through often violent means. Hence, Niebuhr
thinks that Christians may undertake violent action as a requirement of justice, and that there is no final inconsistency between
justice and the use of deadly force.[34]

This brief comparison of Yoder and Niebuhr has shown that
descriptions of justice may have profound importance for the
material commitments of a moral project. They may both reflect
and guide the formulation of substantive positions. On Yoder's

view of justice, any use of violence is clearly unjust. For Niebuhr, violence may be just. Yoder's view requires pacifism; Niebuhr's clearly does not. As the discussion has indicated, moral descriptions are profoundly important for constructing a view of what the Christian life entails.

In our discussion thus far, it should be clear that Yoder has displayed the implications of justice in a way superior to Niebuhr. Yoder believes that the same Jesus who was crucified is now the risen Lord who has begun a new age and who will redeem the universe and fulfill history. Therefore, Yoder is able to interpret the significance of human behavior in line with the eschatological narrative, the key to which is Jesus' example, and especially his acceptance of the cross. That example is one of committed, bold, risky struggle for the kingdom that leads to death and resurrection. Jesus' ethic is not, then, impossible for Yoder; instead, it is a way that requires accepting the suffering heaped upon God's servants as part of the story of a sinful world that awaits its redemption.

Niebuhr is more concerned with the static inevitability of sin and estrangement than with the temporal location of human existence between Pentecost and Parousia. Due to that priority, he fails to see the eschatological narrative in light of which discipleship becomes the proper mode of life. Because he takes Jesus' moral relevance as an impossible ideal, the operative term of Christian ethics becomes a principle of justice not materially informed by Jesus' ministry. Hence, the following of Jesus in nonviolent ministry ceases to be paradigmatic for Christians.

The task of the Christian life is not so much discipleship for Niebuhr as it is accommodation to the structures of human existence in a world not destined for redemption, a world in which there is no foretaste of the kingdom. Undergirding Niebuhr's approach to ethics is the lack of a proper systematic awareness of the eschatological narrative of hope created by Jesus' resurrection. That awareness should shape descriptions of what the Christian life entails.

As a result of the divergence sketched above, Yoder and Niebuhr also have different views of the moral rationality appropriate to the Christian life. For Yoder, Christian moral reason has the task of discerning how to follow Jesus, how to imitate him as a paradigm in the new age within the context of a storied world. For Niebuhr, it has the task of pursuing the responsible use of power in society. Yoder's view of justice, which requires non-violence, is produced through a mode of moral rationality which seeks to figure out what faithfulness to Jesus entails. Niebuhr's view of justice allows for violence in the struggle for balances of power; it is the product of his rationality of responsibility in a world in which faithfulness to Jesus is impossible.

At base, we see here two fundamentally different views of the Christian life, which reflect two distinct eschatologies. Yoder describes ethics in accord with the future created by Jesus' resurrection, while Niebuhr frames moral analysis as guided by a nontemporal view of God's kingdom as an ideal standard of love. Yoder shapes a view of discipleship for which the community of faith is of profound importance; Niebuhr produces an individualistic ethic of intuitive approximation and sees the following of Jesus as an impossible and inappropriate goal.[35]

Attention to their descriptions of moral rationality and moral terms serves to highlight the distinction between them at both theoretical (descriptions of justice) and practical levels (casuistry on Christian participation in violence). It also displays the importance of understanding the Christian life in a manner consistent with the temporal expectation created by Jesus' resurrection. Properly serving the risen Lord requires describing reality in light of the eschatological story of salvation that is grounded in his resurrection. In other words, Christians must acknowledge the importance of their location within God's salvific narrative in order to pursue faithfulness to the risen Lord.

Nevertheless, we note that the moral rationality of discipleship is not without points of commonality and continuity with approaches to moral reason that do not claim to be Christian. Keeping in mind MacIntyre's argument that there are "contested justices, contested rationalities," we need to examine how Christians might respond to views of justice that are not articulated in explicitly Christian terms.[36] Christians should describe the content of moral terms and the task of practical reason as part of our eschatological grasp of reality. In order to do that well, we must be able to respond critically to, and to learn from, projects that conceive the moral life differently.

This is an especially important task for Christians who wish to bring their views of norms, such as justice, into the public arena of moral discourse. Virtually all Christians cooperate in various social endeavors with non-Christians, and many wish to argue against certain construals of moral terms in a way that is intelligible to a non-Christian audience. We therefore simply must give critical attention to the relationship between Christian moral discourse and that of other traditions and communities.

L. Gregory Jones frames the issue in a provocative light in his essay "Should Christians Affirm Rawl's Justice as Fairness?"

> The most important task for Christians committed to justice . . . is to sustain the practices of justice which are in our heritage: feeding the hungry, clothing the naked, serving the widow, ensuring that people of all nations have access to essential "primary goods," and the like. Such activity is central to Christian life, and we ought to participate in those practices which will enable the virtue of justice to flourish.[37]

An important implication of Jones's claim is that a Christian appraisal of other views of justice must be firmly rooted in a way of discipleship that displays justice. This conclusion requires a praxis that manifests "discriminating patterns to judge" whether other views of justice, and the traditions and practices which sustain them, are compatible with or helpful to our pursuit of justice as a necessary quality for discipleship.[38]

Given the unique role of the church as a foretaste of God's justice, Jones is correct in his claim that

> Christians should not turn primarily to the state in the hopes of finding a way to secure justice; what Christians should seek is to sustain those social practices . . . which might form people in the virtues necessary for us to be a just people. It is more likely that Christians will be able to support justice through the witness of doing just activities than by a "theory" of justice.[39]

From within this praxis context of pursuing justice, Christians may examine various secular accounts of justice, whether Rawls's "justice as fairness" or Walzer's "particularism." They can seek to determine whether these constructs illumine the community's quest to embody social relations appropriate to a foretaste of God's kingdom.[40]

Such examination is a task of the practical reason which seeks to guide faithfulness to the risen Lord. As such, it is not, to cite MacIntyre, a search for "a perfect theory, one necessarily to be assented to by any rational being, . . . but rather the best theory to emerge so far in the history of this class of theories."[41] In this instance, the class of theories would be accounts of justice that Christians find helpful for understanding more fully what proper human relations require in a particular instance.

An underlying assumption of this counsel is that justice is not primarily a matter of theory. Instead, it is a quality to be embodied and observed, a trait that we abstract from its display simply for reasons of conceptual analysis. Justice is that quality characteristic of proper human relations in a world to be redeemed by the risen Lord. Hence, justice is a dimension of discipleship, of the practice of following Jesus. Christians should respond to other views of justice from the standpoint of that praxis, through the discernment of the community that seeks to pursue faithfulness to the risen Lord.

Friesen displays how this procedure might work in his examination of Rawls, of "Marxist-Socialist" views of justice, of the rationality of human-rights language, and of merit, free-market, and utilitarian construals. From his reading of Deuteronomy 15:4 and Luke 4:18-19, he states that

> God's justice, which we are to pattern our lives after, is distributed particularly to the disadvantaged or the most undeserving . . . in order to bring about their salvation or wholeness. Poverty, oppression, slavery, and other forms of human deprivation are fundamentally alien to God's compassion for all human beings.[42]

Friesen faults Rawls for an overly individualistic account of justice which cannot take account of the social structures that produce disadvantaged groups. Their plight may be addressed effectively only on a structural level.[43] Likewise, he applauds the socialist emphasis on establishing "a basic social minimum" for "food, clothing, shelter, education," and appropriate employment. Friesen thinks that such patterns of response provide a way to pursue "Christian compassion . . . [and to] care for the fatherless or motherless, the widow, the poor, and the stranger within the community."[44] In addition, Friesen criticizes merit, market, and utilitarian views of justice for being insufficiently focused on meeting the needs of the poor.[45]

Friesen's method in this analysis is to establish a basic Christian conception of justice and to hold other views accountable to it, discerning whether they facilitate or hinder its articulation. Such discernment, moreover, takes place on a level of praxis of the sort for which Jones calls. That is, Friesen identifies central practices of discipleship, in this case caring for the needy, and asks whether various views of justice will help Christians in pursuing what they know to be just.

The moral rationality employed by Friesen assumes an ecclesial location. It has a goal of guiding proper imitation of Christ and is an example of the practical discernment of discipleship that discriminates among competing options in following the goal of faithfulness to the risen Lord.[46] Although Friesen's analysis is not exhaustive at either a theological or philosophical level, he models a way in which Christians may critically engage other views of justice on a fundamentally practical level.

Jones and Friesen make convincing cases that the basic aim of discourse on justice is not abstractly theoretical. Instead, it is a practical discourse of sustaining practices of faithfulness to the risen Lord as a sign of God's new age. In this light, Christians should speak of justice in order to help themselves discern more clearly and fully what discipleship entails in a given circumstance. They want to describe rightly what is at stake in human social relations in a world destined for God's full redemption.

This way of thinking about justice is a good example of the kind of moral description and practical rationality appropriate for those who pursue discipleship during the inbreaking of God's reign. Through such description and reason, we may discern what the faithful service of God requires in particular instances in a world which has yet to come under the fulfilled sovereignty of God.

Is Discipleship "Sectarian"?

Our discussion thus far has shown that a proper temporal understanding of eschatology supports a view of Christian ethics as the *communally sustained* task of discerning what discipleship entails in particular circumstances through the exercise of moral description and practical reason. Contrary to popular assumptions, this approach to ethics may attend to matters beyond the boundaries of the community of faith: it need not withdraw from moral discourse concerning social structures other than the church.

To assert the social relevance of such a communitarian method is controversial. The dominant mode of Christian ethics in this century draws on Ernst Troeltsch's conclusion in *The Social Teaching of the Christian Churches*. It holds that views of the Christian life which emphasize the moral uniqueness of the church and of the task of discipleship are "sectarian" in the sense of being withdrawn from the moral complexity of life in the "real world" for the sake of maintaining the purity of their witness to Jesus.[1]

Troeltsch's Church-Sect Distinction

Troeltsch formulates his famous distinction between the church, sect, and mystic types in a fashion that makes the church type the only form of Christian social existence which may fulfill his view of the proper end of Christian ethics. It alone provides resources for answering his question: "How can the church harmonize with these main forces [state and society] in such a way that together they will form a unity of civilization?" He thinks that sects combine Jesus' radical ethic with an absolute view of natural law. Taken together, the two are so rigorous and unrealistic in their expectations for human behavior that withdrawal from the relativities and complexities of culture is the sects' only alternative.[2]

Friesen, in his article "Normative Factors in Troeltsch's Typology of Religious Association," perceives that behind Troeltsch's distinction between church and sect is a view of

> religion as "idea" [which] refers to a transcendental realm beyond the relativities of culture. . . . The religious "idea" of Christianity, being at first purely religious and in opposition to culture, must then be synthesized with culture. By definition the rational core of religion is distinct from culture. This distinction between the *a priori* and the actual involves a fundamental duality that initially sets religion and culture in opposition to each other.[3]

According to Friesen, Troeltsch sees religion as requiring a polarity between the individual and the social:

> Religion is first of all a direct and individual relationship to the suprasensible or divine spirit. Only secondarily is religion a sociocultural phenomenon connected with a particular religious community or tradition.

Thus Friesen thinks that Troeltsch's view of religion "presupposes an individualistic mysticism," which interacts with social forces to produce different cultural forms of religious belief and practice.[4]

This mysticism is of a piece with Troeltsch's individualistic view of the basic ethic of the gospel as

(1) the religious idea of the Presence of God which is conceived as a searching and penetrating gaze and as a "fascination" which draws men [and women] to Himself; and (2) the thought of the infinite and the eternal value of the soul to be attained through self-renunciation for the sake of God.[5]

Even as the moral essence of Christianity does not concern directly the social realities of life, God's kingdom is not compatible with them. Instead, the kingdom

> is an ideal which requires a new world if it is to be fully realized; it was this new world-order that Jesus proclaimed in His message of the Kingdom of God. But it is an ideal which cannot be realized within the world apart from compromise. Therefore, the history of the Christian Ethos becomes the story of a constantly renewed search for this compromise and of fresh opposition to this spirit of compromise.[6]

Friesen comments that a crucial factor in Troeltsch's approval of "the church type [is that it] . . . seeks a compromise between the original eschatological vision and the various historical situations" in which Christians find themselves. Indeed, the

> fundamental difference between [church and sect] . . . is that the sect type continues to reaffirm the ideal eschatological utopian vision which by definition orients it "beyond" the world, whereas the church type continually seeks to compromise this vision by relating the ideal to the social situation of the world.[7]

According to Friesen, there is a "striking similarity" between Troeltsch's view of the relationship between church and world and that of Luther: "Troeltsch's own categories are a modernized version of the basic dualities present in Luther's doctrine of the two kingdoms." Luther distinguished between the inner dispositions of faith and love as the direct concern of God's kingdom and the harsh requirements of social situations in the world. Troeltsch

> also operates with a duality which on the one hand stresses the very personal and inward values of the Christian faith, but on the

> other hand emphasizes a very realistic and pessimistic view of the external structure of society where the impersonal norm of law and justice operates. . . . The problem for Luther and Troeltsch is similar: How is it possible to bring together a mystical sense of religion with a thoroughgoing realism with respect to the world?[8]

Friesen's argument demonstrates that "Troeltsch's typology of religious association is not only a descriptive sociological model, but also a normative model which reflects . . . [a] preference for the church type."[9] On this point, Troeltsch is not an "objective" social scientist who presents the "facts" about Christian social life. In his formulation of the church-sect distinction, he is primarily a theologian who makes a case for one ecclesiology over others because the church type alone meets the standards produced by his prior theological commitments.

Historians or sociologists of religion might argue with Troeltsch about the adequacy of his reading of patterns of social behavior among Christians in various times and places. Yet it is important that we engage him *theologically* in order to examine and critique the substantive commitments implicit in his preference for the church type and its ethic of compromise. In so doing, it will become clear that the church-sect distinction is a descriptive strategy which reflects problematic theological assumptions.

In particular, Troeltsch's essentially individualistic view of the gospel and his construal of the present moral relevance of God's kingdom appear to be symptoms of inadequate eschatological commitments which are of a piece with his church-sect typology. He understands Christian ethics as the task of working compromises between the pure religion of the individual and the corrupting social realities of life. Thereby he fails to see that the Christian life is the fundamentally social undertaking of manifesting a foretaste of God's kingdom. It means pursuing faithfulness to the risen Lord in God's good but rebellious creation, which is destined for final redemption.

As the discussion of 1 Corinthians made clear in the second chapter, the individual Christian is radically contextualized by location within the community which is a foretaste of the kingdom. Particular Christians are parts of the body of Christ, produced and sustained through its practices. Indeed, the pursuit of discipleship is unintelligible apart from that social context. The substance of discipleship is the active following of Jesus; this undertaking requires a continual communal formation and discernment in order to help the Christian see what discipleship entails in particular instances.

To the extent that Troeltsch assumes an individualistic essence of Christian ethics that is more basic than the social location of the church, he obscures the centrality of the community of faith for the task of discipleship.[10] He assumes a false dichotomy between the individual and the social that leads to an ethic of compromise. Thus his formulation distorts the task of Christian ethics as the communal pursuit of faithfulness to the risen Lord.

Moreover, Troeltsch views God's kingdom as an ideal realm from which the individual is estranged in the social ambiguities of history. This is in tension with the logic of Christian eschatological expectation. Because of Jesus' resurrection, the fulfillment of God's kingdom is a future event which is to be foreshadowed now in the social life of the church by the power of the Spirit. Christians should see themselves within an eschatological narrative of redemption, between Pentecost and Parousia, in which their task is to pursue faithfulness to the risen Lord.

With Troeltsch, one may speak of the Christian life primarily as an exercise of compromising the demands of an individualistic gospel in line with the sinful realities of social orders. If we do that, we fail to see that a dialectic between the individual and the social is not what is primarily at stake here theologically. What is at stake is the question of whether human existence, in both its individual and social aspects, will display proper faithfulness to the Lord, in whose future lies the destiny of all reality.

Again, one may with Troeltsch speak of the kingdom as an ideal realm apparently incapable of realization in history. Such talk describes an aspect of reality as timelessly estranged, not as a realm created by God and to be redeemed by the God known in Jesus, the God who demands present faithfulness. It means that the social conditions of historical existence preclude discipleship and demand compromise in a way that obscures the location of all reality within the temporal narrative of God's creation and redemption.

In contrast to Troeltsch, our discussion shows that, in this God's storied domain, proper human relations require the characteristics of discipleship. The Christ who calls us to follow him is the agent of both our creation and redemption. We live in this God's domain, in which the possibility of faithfulness may not be ruled out. Hence, it is problematic to speak of a realm of human existence, such as the social, which is necessarily or inevitably estranged from the right service of God.

Contrasting Yoder with Troeltsch on this point presses the issue. Yoder sees the community of faith located within an eschatological scheme that demands present faithfulness in the midst of a sinful world. He wants to reject Troeltsch's position that compromise in order to sustain a civilization is the most appropriate social strategy for Christians. Yoder rejects Troeltsch's formulation of the individual and social polarity on the grounds of his communitarian view of the Christian life. He therefore has no trouble speaking of the church as the proper social locus of faith, the entity that pursues a communal imitation of Christ.[11]

In this regard, compromise with the world is a notion incompatible with the practical reason of discipleship. If the goal of moral discernment is to guide faithfulness to the risen Lord, to manifest a foretaste of the kingdom, it is not consistent with that goal to describe the task of the Christian life as compromise with the sinful realities of the world. For Yoder, communal faithfulness is possible, and it is the necessary goal of the Christian life. For Troeltsch, that sort of faithfulness fails to satisfy the need for an ethic to sustain a civilization, and hence it is inappropriate. By Troeltsch's logic of an ethic of compromise, faithfulness does not make sense and does not pursue the perferred goal. Yoder and Troeltsch have, then, profoundly different understandings of the Christian life.

Yoder points to the basis of his disagreement with Troeltsch in "The Constantinian Sources of Western Social Ethics." He argues that with Constantine's conversion the church ceased to be a distinct, minority social structure and became synonymous with the dominant governmental and cultural order. Hence, "the meaning of the word *Christian* has changed. Its moral, emotional, and even intellectual meanings were changed by the reversal of the sociological and political pressures."

Indeed, with Christianity as the state religion, the kingdom and "Providence no longer needed to be an object of faith, for God's governance of history had become empirically evident in the person of the Christian ruler of the world." In the "Christian" empire, matters of sustaining the social order took precedence over matters of discipleship. Yoder says, "Ethics had to change because one must aim one's behavior at strengthening the regime. . . . The conception of a distinctive lifestyle befitting Christian confession had to be sweepingly redefined" in a way compatible with the exigencies of the empire.[12]

In accord with Troeltsch's typology, some churches are called "sectarian," because they put a goal of faithfulness over that of compromise. Such a description is dependent upon the "Constantinian" commitment that the church is a social institution which exists primarily for the sustenance or enrichment of the larger society. In this view, the most profound identification of the Christian is with the dominant social order. The use of the term *sectarian* implies that its speaker identifies with a larger social structure. From this perspective, other groups are described as marginal because they do not participate in the programs or goals of that order, and they resist identification with it.[13]

The logic of this description entails the belief that the church is but one social structure within a larger societal matrix through which God's purposes are known. Advocates of this view primarily see continuity and consistency between the gospel and the dominant culture. The great problem with this approach to ethics, as Yoder points out, is that the nature of Christian belief and practice must change when the goal of moral reasoning becomes the sustenance of such a social order.

Certainly, Troeltsch recognizes this fact in his talk of an ethic of compromise. To hold the Christian life accountable to the support of a secular political regime, an economic system, a military force, or a cultural milieu, will surely alter the shape of the lifestyle appropriate to those who seek to embody God's coming kingdom rather than the rebellious kingdoms of the world.

Yoder states, for example, that in the time of Charlemagne "the name of Jesus is now intoned over a Germanic culture without changing its inner content, as it had been intoned over Greco-Roman culture for half a millennium before."[14] Whenever people invoke the risen Lord as a means of uncritical support for an empire, they subvert the nature of the lordship of a Messiah who demanded that his followers subordinate all other loyalties to their loyalty to him. They obscure the tension between the demands of God's kingdom and the exigencies of the kingdoms of the world who crucified our Lord.

In "Constantinian" theology, the church ceases to have an ethic or goal distinct from that of the larger society. The Christian community comes to see itself located within a narrative of "God and Country." God's kingdom is thought to be present, at least in a compromised sense, throughout the national social order. Hence, the church loses its unique identity as the foretaste of God's reign, as a storied fellowship which is to embody proleptically the coming consummation of a kingdom not of this world, a kingdom which challenges the often idolatrous claims of rebellious political orders.

Apart from this eschatological location, the practical reason of the Christian life ceases to be that of a discipleship which pursues faithfulness. It becomes a means of compromise with and advancement of the dominant order, the social structure that supposedly manifests God's will for human relations. From the perspective of the "Constantinian" ethicist, churches which pursue faithfulness over compromise will appear to be sectarian. They will seem to be socially irrelevant, withdrawn communities due to their refusal to cooperate in the sustenance of God's societywide order and their failure to accept their primary task as that of joining with other social institutions for the enrichment of the commonwealth.

The *sectarian* classification, however, rests on problematic theological assumptions: (1) The church is *not* the unique foretaste of God's kingdom through the power of the Spirit. (2) Providence has identified secular political structures as the embodiment of God's reign. (3) The task of discipleship must be construed in a way compatible with the demands of sustaining the dominant order.

The crux of the problem is that those assumptions are in severe tension with central aspects of Christian belief. They refuse to see the church as the peculiar social manifestation of the future guaranteed by Jesus' resurrection. They fail to regard the Christian life as the communally sustained task of pursuing faithfulness to the risen Lord in a sinful world.

In the essay "A People in the World," Yoder makes a lucid critique of Troeltsch on this point. He develops an alternative typology of forms of the Christian community: "Theocrats" seek societal reform in the name of God in a way analogous to Troeltsch's church type. "Spiritualists" have an essentially inward view of the Christian life in a way similar to the mystic type. "Believers church" Christians seek to develop forms of social organization "which are according to Scripture and which are expressive of the character of the disciples' fellowship." Yoder clearly intends this third category as a more appropriate way of describing the congregational forms of Christianity that Troeltsch rejected as sects.[15]

Against essentially individualistic views of the gospel, such as that of Troeltsch, Yoder declares the following:

> The creation of one new humanity [in the church] by breaking down the wall between the two kinds of people of whom the world is made, Jews and Gentiles, is not simply the result of reconciliation of individuals with God. . . . This creation of the one new humanity is itself the purpose which God had in all ages, is itself the "mystery," the gospel to be proclaimed. In every direction we might follow in this exposition, the distinctiveness of the church of believers is prerequisite to the meaningfulness of the gospel message.[16]

Indeed, the believers church is "the miracle of the new humanity" in its actual demonstration of an alternative social order to the fallen, divisive ways of the world. The existence of this kind of community is vital for the very proclamation of the gospel. "There can be no evangelistic call addressed to a person inviting him [or her] to enter a new kind of fellowship and learning if there is not such a body of persons. . . ."

Yoder also claims that the believers church differs from the

theocrats and spiritualists in its belief that the church should be
"a discerning community," the social structure necessary for describing well God's action and requirements in history.

> The promise of the presence of the Holy Spirit is clearly correlat-
> ed in the New Testament with the need for the church, propheti-
> cally to discern right and wrong in the events of the age. Not all
> visible events are God at work, not all "action" is divine, not every
> Spirit is of Christ. . . . The church is qualified to be such an agent
> of discernment . . . because she has in her allegiance to Jesus
> Christ criteria of good and evil which are significantly different
> from those which prevail in even the most respectable segments
> of the larger society.[17]

Yoder sees that the gospel has an intrinsic social nature. Thus
he frames an approach to Christian ethics which works out the
implications of discipleship without assuming a corrupting polarity between the individual and the social. The problematic is
not that of translating the ideal individual religious experience
into a foreign social sphere. Hence, Yoder presents an alternative to Troeltsch which rightly makes the Christian life a matter
of pursuing a communally sustained faithfulness.

Likewise, Yoder makes the point that the believers church
should be characterized by a social ethic of holy living, a manner
of behaving that displays the implications of discipleship in a
way distinct from the actions and standards of others. He is
against an ethic of compromise:

> The need is for what they do in the world to be different because
> they are Christian; to be a reflection not merely of their restored
> self-confidence nor of their power to set the course of society but
> of the social novelty of the covenant of grace. Instead of doing,
> each in his [or her] own station or office, whatever any reasonable
> person would do in the same place according to the order of cre-
> ation, the need is for what he [or she] does there to be judged and
> renewed by the difference which it makes that Christ, and not
> mammon or Mars, is his [or her] Lord.[18]

In addition, the believers church will embody a discipline that
seeks to reconcile the erring member because of love for one

another. It must also witness to those outside the community in a fashion characterized more strongly by fidelity to the demands of the gospel than to those of popularity. Similarly, its members will accept the suffering that its witness may evoke at the hands of the dominant order.

> Thus willingness to bear the cross means simply the readiness to let the form of the church's obedience to Christ be dictated by Christ rather than by how much the population or the authorities are ready to accept. . . . The readiness of the church to face suffering thus understood is precisely the only way in which it is possible to communicate to that society and to its authorities that it is Christ who is Lord and not they.[19]

Yoder's typology of theocrat, spiritualist, and believers church is superior to Troeltsch's description of the forms of Christian social organization. This is the case because Yoder's typology performs the theologically justified function of allowing an ecclesiology of church as foretaste of the kingdom to be described in a way that is not marginal to God's purposes in history or removed from the work of Providence in the world.

For Yoder, those who pursue communal faithfulness are believers in the gospel whose social arrangements and moral life reflect their fidelity to the risen Lord. For Troeltsch, such Christians are sectarians, who stray from the goal of sustaining a civilization. Yoder's typology allows three distinct ecclesiologies to be held accountable to the theological logic which makes the idea of a church intelligible. According to that logic, Yoder rightly finds the believers church to be most appropriate. That view identifies the church temporally as the unique social locus of faithfulness to the risen Lord, whose relations with other social structures should be characterized more by conflict than by continuity. Christian eschatological convictions support Yoder's view of the task of the Christian life as discipleship, and deny the theological adequacy of Troeltsch's ethic of compromise and of his typology, which serves to underwrite his ethic.

There is another way of putting my preference for *believers church* over *sect*. We live in a world created by God and to be redeemed by God. That same God requires our faithfulness in the present. Therefore, discipleship simply may not be described as marginal from what is truly important in history and society. On the basis of Christian belief, the most significant aspect of human existence is our service of the God incarnate in Jesus. There is no Christian theological ground from which someone may argue that such service in this God's universe, in which a new age has already begun because of Jesus' resurrection, is withdrawn from or irrelevant to that which is ultimately important, meaningful, or true.

The followers of Troeltsch see this style of community-centered discipleship as sectarian because they have failed to describe the universe in its entirety as the domain of the risen Lord, who requires faithfulness and not compromise. As "Constantinians," they interpret their faith in a way that allows a stronger identification with the dominant social order than with the church as a unique social locus of discipleship. They see Providence embodied more fully in the larger social order than in the witness of the church. Christian ethics thereby becomes accommodated to the demands of sustaining an empire or civilization. Compromise takes precedence over discipleship. In the storied universe of which the God known in Jesus is both Creator and Redeemer, that move is problematic; it holds the service of God accountable to the service of a sinful world.

At stake in the competing typologies of Troeltsch and Yoder are important theological, and at base eschatological, commitments. The distinction between sect and believers church is not a simple matter of "objective" description. Instead, it depends on profound theological commitments which warrant the descriptions. Troeltsch reflects "Constantinian" sensibilities; Yoder, in light of temporal eschatological expectation, emphasizes the moral distinctiveness which is incumbent upon the church as a foretaste of God's coming kingdom.

Gustafson's Temptation

James Gustafson, a contemporary ethicist, has followed Troeltsch in advancing a problematic account of "sectarianism." In "The Sectarian Temptation: Reflections on Theology, the Church, and the University," he argues that communitarian moral projects wrongly assume "a kind of Christian tribe living in a kind of ghetto whose members are (or can be) shaped . . . almost exclusively by the biblical or Christian language or narratives."

Gustafson thinks that views of the Christian life which emphasize the centrality of the church as a social locus for moral formation rely exclusively on particularistic theological claims. As a result, they may neither incorporate aspects of worldly wisdom nor address secular matters such as economics, politics, or medicine.[20] Our discussion will show that Gustafson is wrong to assert that communitarian projects are necessarily withdrawn from such matters. His formulation reflects inadequate theological, and especially eschatological, assumptions.

Gustafson declares that "faithful witness to Jesus is not a sufficient theological and moral basis for addressing the moral and social problems of the twentieth century."[21] Behind this assertion stands his view that God is "the sustainer and even destroyer of aspects of life in the world," especially through the forces of nature. Therefore, theological statements must "be informed by investigations proper to nature" in order to speak well of God's purposes and the proper human response to God.[22]

Hence, theologians should address moral problems

> as an outcome of a theology that develops God's relations to all aspects of life in the world, and develops those relations in terms which are not exclusively Christian in a sectarian form. Jesus is not God.[23]

Gustafson thinks that viewing Christian ethics as the task of discerning how to follow Jesus in a distinct community of faithfulness amounts to "sectarian" moral reasoning. It is a surrender to the temptation to withdraw morally, theologically, and intellectually from the complexities of life in the contemporary world.[24]

A first line of response to Gustafson concerns his charge that

> in sectarian Christian form God becomes a Christian God for Christian people. . . . God is assumed to be the tribal God of a minority of the earth's population.[25]

Hence, moral concern does not extend beyond the boundaries of the community.

We respond to Gustafson by demonstrating the interrelation of Christian claims about creation, Christology, and eschatology. Gustafson charges that communitarian projects advance a withdrawal ethic which compartmentalizes the moral life and ignores social realities other than the church. His argument does not, however, take account of the basic Christian affirmation that the same Lord whom Christians seek to follow is the agent of the creation of the entire universe: "All things came into being through him, and without him not one thing came into being" (John 1:3). The Christ is

> the firstborn of all creation; for in him all things in heaven and on earth were created, things visible and invisible, whether thrones or dominions or rulers or powers—all things have been created through him and for him. (Col. 1:15-16)

Thus the same Lord who will subject all things to the Father in the eschaton is also the agent of their creation. Christians must therefore view the world as God's good but rebellious realm, destined for final redemption. Throughout that world we may properly pursue discipleship. The one in whom we hope is the same Lord through whom all reality came into existence. Hence, there is no radical discontinuity of a narrow realm of discipleship and a larger alien realm created by a god not known in Jesus. Instead, there is one universe, created by one God and to be fulfilled by the same.

The church has the task of being that part of the created order in which the right submission to God that will characterize the eschaton is proleptically manifest. As argued in the second chapter, it is only by participation in the life of the church that Christians may be formed and sustained properly as disciples able to discern the particulars of the Christian life in a rebellious world. Yet Christians stand within God's domain whether they are operating in the social sphere of church, which is never entirely free from corruption, or in the sphere of the rebellious world. No aspect of creation is essentially foreign territory to the

Christian who seeks to serve the Creator and Redeemer of the universe. Hence, our ethic does not necessarily entail an isolated withdrawal into the confines of the community of faith.

Neither does our emphasis on the moral relevance of the church require the thoroughgoing sociological withdrawal described by Gustafson. We maintain that Christians are free to participate in aspects of social life outside the community if those aspects are consistent with the task of discipleship. Both conscientious abstinence and participation in extraecclesial affairs may be appropriate, depending on the nature of the particular endeavor. Through the moral formation entailed by the communal practices of discipleship, Christians may develop skills to deal critically with opportunities for participation in the diverse social structures of the world.

We recognize that the nonchurch realm is not an entirely evil reality from which Christians must flee. Hence, the community of faith may focus its descriptive attention and practical rationality on the extraecclesial matters which it judges to be proper opportunities for the ministry of the gospel. Likewise, individual Christians may pursue ministry within nonchurch social structures so long as they do so in a manner consistent with the communally sustained task of discipleship.

It is fitting for Christians, in certain times and places, to participate selectively in various governmental and economic institutions. Their purpose can be to play a role in guiding them in ways that are in keeping with the demands of God's inbreaking reign. The particulars of such participation will be worked out through the discernment of the community and of the individual Christian who continues to be formed through the practices of the community. Such practical reason is a process undertaken in the midst of the praxis of seeking faithfulness to the risen Lord in the power of the Spirit. As a Spirit-enabled discernment, it is not the work of a supposedly autonomous reason which tries to achieve its own salvation.

In a similar way, Christians may incorporate into their intellectual and moral projects sources of wisdom, such as philosophy or the social and natural sciences, which are not basically theological. In doing so, they must interpret and employ these sources in a way which illuminates the pursuit of the Christian life.[26] All objects and modes of knowledge exist within the one realm that God has created and will fulfill in the eschaton. Therefore, no sort of discourse is necessarily ruled out as a proper source of knowledge for Christians. It is a matter of the church's discernment what particular fonts of knowledge will be helpful for its task at particular times. That judgment requires the sustenance of communal procedures of moral formation, so that disciples will be able to determine when and how to incorporate such discourses.

This reference to a doctrine of creation is not an attempt to provide a theological basis for a universalized moral language on which all people, by virtue of their status as God's creatures, may agree. Neither is it a theological justification for a moral realm outside the lordship of Jesus. Instead, it is an attempt to show why communitarian ethics does not require withdrawal from areas of life other than the church. Precisely because of the interrelation of beliefs about Christology, creation, and eschatology, disciples may view all creation as the domain of God. In and through that domain, they may properly pursue the Christian life in accord with their communal formation.

Let us take the response to Gustafson a step further. It is a mistake for him to hold that the task of moral analysis in the twentieth century is simply too complex to allow an ethic of discipleship to guide Christian discernment. His point is based on problematic assumptions about the task and method of Christian theology and discipleship. He employs the notion that "theology has to be open to all the sources that help us to construe God's relations to the world; ethics has to deal with the interdependence of all things in relation to God." Then he proceeds in a fashion which privileges the insights of secular discourse, especially natural science, over traditional claims about the centrality of Jesus Christ for faith and practice.[27]

Thus Gustafson gives priority to the discourse of scientists in the academy over the practical discernment of the community of faith. Indeed, he affirms aspects of Christian theological tradition only if they are justified by "important and appropriate experiences and perceptions of the human condition in relation to the Other" as those are known through scientific inquiry.[28]

In Gustafson's view, God is

> the power that bears down upon us, sustains us, sets an ordering of relationships, provides conditions and possibilities for human activity and even a sense of direction. The evidence from various sciences suggest the plausibility of viewing God in these terms.[29]

Jesus is basically an example of proper ordering before God. He "incarnates theocentric piety and fidelity . . . [as] a historical embodiment of what we are to be and to do—indeed, of what God is enabling and requiring us to be and to do."[30]

Gustafson understands redemption to entail an

> ordering of not only our individual motives and desires but also of the natural and social world in light of what can be perceived and interpreted about the proper relations of things to each other and finally of divine governance.[31]

Likewise, Christian moral discernment requires the agent to "enlarge" his or her view of values, purposes, and goals that are operative in nature and society, and to order the self in relation to them in a manner appropriate to their relations with God.[32]

Here is the crux of the matter: According to Gustafson, the clearest knowledge of God's purposes comes through a broadly construed reading of the "signs of the times" which assumes that whatever happens is the work of God. Thus Gustafson cannot focus ethics on the task of discerning how to follow Jesus as a Messiah who modeled a particular way of life in his ministry and called disciples to follow him in definite patterns of activity. Gustafson's broader approach to ethics takes as its most determining source what God is doing today as that is known through natural and social sciences. In Gustafson's view, God is the sum of the powers and forces of the universe. Hence, the sciences, identified by Gustafson as the most appropriate means of knowledge about those powers and forces, provide the most direct access to what God would have us do and who God would have us be.

Gustafson thinks that Jesus models this way of proper ordering before God. He thereby reduces Jesus' life to an example of theocentric piety without displaying what material relevance Jesus' particular teachings and actions should have for those who seek to follow him.[33] Gustafson's lack of specificity about Jesus' example reflects his effort to focus attention on what the sciences tell us that God is doing now, not on how a figure of ancient history proclaimed the kingdom of God.

With this analysis, I allow Gustafson's recent "theocentric" orientation to supersede his earlier systematic work. His 1968 book *Christ and the Moral Life* presents Jesus as "a common object of loyalty" for Christians. In light of his example, Christians should "form their intentions." Jesus is "the norm for the Christian's theological interpretation of what God wills that life should be . . . [and] of what the Christian ought to be and to do. . . ."[34] With his 1981 first volume of *Ethics from a Theocentric Perspective*, Gustafson tempers claims about the centrality of Jesus and denies his divinity and the adequacy of an ethic of discipleship. He has little concern to display in precise terms how Jesus is materially relevant for the Christian life. According to Gustafson's later theocentric perspective, Jesus is not crucial for the right knowledge of God's purposes.[35]

Thus the cultural and moral complexity of the twentieth century is for Gustafson the work of God, the doing of Providence. The most important questions for Christians to ask are these: What is God enabling, directing, and requiring in this or that event, movement, or discovery? How should I respond to this phenomenon in a manner appropriate to its and my relation to God?

Since Gustafson favors this way of knowing God's purposes, he finds inadequate a discipleship ethic which assumes that God is paradigmatically revealed and indeed incarnated in Jesus. He rejects such a model of revelation that takes priority over other ways of knowing God and that requires participation in a community of disciples in order for God's purposes to be known well. Gustafson refuses to base Christian ethics on following someone who was rightly pious two thousand years ago. He sees that as ignoring what the Sovereign is doing now, for the sake of reproducing how Jesus responded to what the Sovereign did long ago. For Gustafson, such a move is wrongly traditionalistic, more concerned with "maintaining fidelity to the biblical narratives about Jesus" than with seeing all things in relation to God.[36]

An important logical step in the construction of Gustafson's project is his rejection of Jesus' resurrection and the temporal eschatological hope that hinges upon it:

> We may not be able to say what the end will be, but, as Troeltsch stated, it will not be the Apocalypse of traditional Christian thought. . . . If our perceptions of the Deity are in and through nature and human experience, and what is imaged is a divine governance of the world, then the biblical eschatological symbols or the contemporary Christian developments of them are not sustainable.[37]

Like much of his project, this statement relies on the findings of natural science. Gustafson dismisses the Christian belief in the resurrection of the one person, Jesus of Nazareth, almost two thousand years ago as the beginning of the redemption of the world. He thinks that particular belief is not consistent with what scientists tell us about how nature works.

Gustafson's refusal to accept an eschatological view of reality is of a piece with his repudiation of communitarian approaches to Christian ethics. Since he denies that a new age of God's reign was initiated with Jesus' resurrection, he has no reason to be especially concerned with any particular community as a foretaste of that age through the power of the Spirit. The powers bear down upon, sustain, and finally destroy all people alike. There is no unique role of the church in relation to God's kingdom; location in the church is not necessary for discerning what the service of God entails.

Gustafson's most determining theological claim is that God acts upon us through the plethora of powers which we encounter in life. Hence, to privilege the social reality of the church is to denigrate the great majority of powers and forces through which God is known, indeed, which are God. With Gustafson's view of Jesus as simply an example of piety, not the risen Lord, it becomes dubious to speak of him as a Messiah whom Christians should seek to follow via a community proleptically embodying the kingdom which he will consummate.

Moreover, Gustafson describes reality primarily in terms of the findings of natural science. He holds traditional Christian formulations accountable to the findings of science. Thus, he treats the discoveries of science as key hermeneutical points, virtually ahistorical statements of truth, which form a paradigm for the interpretation of all other discourse. That move is theologically askew for Christians because it denies the legitimacy of a central claim of Christian faith: the particular narrative assertion that God has performed a unique deed in Jesus' resurrection which is grounds for hope in a future warranted on the basis of that act, and not on the basis of "objective" scientific analysis. Gustafson's method collapses the eschatological story of God's salvific activity into a static scientific reading of reality. That precludes the hope of Christians for a new age, for a future fulfillment of the universe.[38]

For Gustafson, God is not the Sovereign who creates and will redeem in freedom and who wills to be active in human history. Instead, God is the impersonal "divine governance" without agency, intention, or volition.[39] Gustafson does not view human history as contextualized by the narrative of God's creation and coming redemption. He does not grant that reality is illuminated by the new age begun in Jesus' resurrection and is the domain of the risen Lord, who requires faithfulness in the present. Such an approach to ethics, from his perspective, describes the universe in traditional theological categories which cannot be sustained by the privileged findings of natural science. These traditional categories rely on the beliefs of a particular historical community and ignore the scientific discourse that Gustafson treats as virtually the absolute, indisputable, and universal font of truth.[40]

Since Gustafson does not describe the world as the storied realm of God's redemption, he is not interested in the particular theological claims that become intelligible from their location in that story. Thus he dispenses with the uniqueness of the church as foretaste of the kingdom and the importance of a discipleship ethic. He has replaced this eschatological reading of reality with the supposedly universal and obviously true discourse of natural science.

Gustafson's theological commitments, then, undergird his rejection of communitarian moral projects which assume the adequacy of a discipleship ethic and the uniqueness of the church. His approach to ethics is theologically problematic on Christological, ecclesial, and eschatological grounds. He denies the basic Christian affirmation that Jesus was declared the Christ through his resurrection. Thus he rejects the very event that began God's new age, in which the church in the power of the Spirit is a foretaste of God's fulfilled reign.[41] Because Gustafson's arguments do not display how communitarian projects are inappropriate implications of the logic of Christian belief, his critique is not persuasive on Christian theological grounds.

Let us respond further to Gustafson's call for Christians to "relate ourselves and all things in a manner appropriate to our, and their, relations to God."[42] In contrast to Gustafson, we hold that believers can do this only by interpreting the events of history and the discoveries of science in light of a temporal eschatological hope in the risen Lord. In terms of his future, Christians see the destiny of all reality. The Jesus whom we follow is not simply an example of piety or a moral teacher; he is the risen Lord, the agent of both creation and redemption, who is present with the church through the power of the Spirit.

An eschatology of hope in the future of the risen Lord calls the church to be a particular community of discipleship, a foretaste of the new age in a world besieged by the forces of sin. Jesus' resurrection has ushered in a qualitatively new age of human existence before God. Therefore, it is incumbent upon those who profess allegiance to Jesus to pursue discipleship through the community that may uniquely foreshadow the fullness of history which the risen Lord will bring.

Gustafson is surely correct in saying that "the understanding and formed convictions that Christians have about God are important for the way in which they discern things morally, and what they actually discern to be morally appropriate." Yet it is crucial to recognize that Gustafson's theological commitments shape a view of the moral life and its discernment which are hardly consistent with the rationale of Christian belief.[43]

In his method, "the human task is to decide what is the morally best possible course of events and state of affairs" through a broad view of the competing values of the natural world as known through scientific enquiry.[44] That discernment requires a sense of piety before God, a piety grounded in the recognition that human well-being is but one among many values. However, Gustafson does not describe the process of moral reason as the task of discerning the pattern of faithfulness to the risen Lord, the God incarnate in Jesus. Jesus' example and teaching provide "poignant exemplifications . . . of what theocentric piety and fidelity call upon us to do." But Jesus is not for Gustafson the Christ whose presence with the church through the Spirit enables the discernment of discipleship as a sign of the new age.[45]

Reality looks different to those who see it in light of Jesus' resurrection; just so should the moral life look different to those who intend discipleship. Since Gustafson does not perceive the universe as destined for redemption because of Jesus' victory over death, he has no reason to view the moral life as the following of the risen Lord in the community that foreshadows God's fulfilled reign. His project therefore misconstrues the task of *Christian* ethics. He calls for the service of a god not incarnate in Jesus, views Jesus as an example of proper piety but not as the risen Lord, and describes a world not destined for God's redemption. Hence, his view obscures the proper task of the Christian life as the communally sustained following of the risen Lord in the new age of God's kingdom. In summary, Gustafson fails to see the centrality of a temporal eschatology for Christian ethics.

Gustafson's approach to ethics, like that of Troeltsch, may be described as "Constantinian." In a nation or society which claims to be Christian, the task of sustaining the social order is typically construed in a fashion which places an ethic of support for the dominant order over an ethic of discipleship. Often this is done because God's reign is thought to be embodied in the nation. For Gustafson, likewise, Providence is embodied in the sum of powers operative in nature and society.[46]

Gustafson takes the complexity of responding to those powers as a justification for rejecting the ethic of discipleship. He favors a mode of moral analysis which is supposedly more amenable to participation in a pluralist society, which itself is the work of Providence. For "Christian" nations the task of sustaining God's ordained social order may take precedence over the calling of discipleship. Even so for Gustafson the task of responding to powers and events takes precedence over following Jesus.[47]

In both schemes, it is wrongly assumed that God is known more clearly through the signs of the times than through the way of faithfulness to God's new age as that is displayed in the ministry of the now risen Lord. These present-day signs may be the establishment of a "Christian" empire or the discoveries of natural science. Both sources supply a view of what God is doing now, by which Jesus' teaching and example are interpreted. This is done in a fashion that distorts the Christian life from its identity as the way of following the risen Lord in the community that partially manifests God's kingdom.

Supporters of "Christian" empires will find that an ethic of discipleship is not sufficient to sustain a worldly kingdom. Just so, Gustafson finds that "faithful witness to Jesus is not a sufficient theological and moral basis for addressing the moral and social problems of the twentieth century."[48] Both formulations imply that what is materially determining for discernment is something other than the task of Christian discipleship.

Indeed, the views of what God is doing now, either through a "Christian" society or the events of nature, are not so much justified theologically as by what seems self-evident in a social order other than the church. There may be a perceived need for a common religion to sustain political control or for a view of science as a means of knowledge that does not need epistemological justification. In either case, both "Constantinianism" and the position of Gustafson hold the Christian life accountable primarily to the discernment of communities of discourse other than the ecclesial structures which have unique resources for the embodiment of God's reign. With such a theological method, it is no wonder that neither way has much concern with the distinctiveness of the church as a locus of moral formation.

In contrast, our eschatologically informed approach to ethics has great concern with the church's role in moral formation precisely because of a theologically based emphasis on the Christian life as the pursuit of discipleship within the context of community. In an important sense, the church continues to face the challenge, to quote Yoder, of "non-empire."[49] In other words, the ecclesial task is to manifest a distinct realm of social organization. In that realm the dominant order may be resisted in accord with God's reign; in and through the church, disciples may learn to serve a Lord who is neither Caesar nor the sum of powers that form the status quo.

Gustafson's approach to ethics does not effectively allow for the sustenance and centrality of such an alternative community. As a result, he succumbs to the temptation to "baptize" uncritically the dominant social order. This is likewise a temptation to see Providence embodied in events and structures in a way that makes the discipleship of Jesus a task largely irrelevant to the real business of life in the world. It transforms the Christian life into an endeavor of sustaining the kingdoms of this world in a way that distorts the eschatological nature of discipleship as an undertaking which finds its intelligibility in the new age begun in Jesus' resurrection.[50]

Gustafson's position does not take account of the identity of the risen Lord as the agent of creation, who will transform the world into a realm of right subjection to God in the eschaton. Since Gustafson holds that an ethic of faithfulness to that Lord is irrelevant for life in God's world, his ethical theory is profoundly problematic for Christians. In effect, he calls us to serve a lord other than the Christ, and to do that in a world which is the domain of a god not incarnate in Jesus. To give in to that temptation is a serious theological mistake. It is much better to understand the task of the Christian life as the discipleship of Jesus in and through the community which has the purpose of proleptically manifesting God's reign.

Medical Ethics

Discipleship is not, as we have argued against Troeltsch and Gustafson, a moral undertaking necessarily insulated and withdrawn from extraecclesial social spheres. The field of medical ethics provides examples of how our communally and eschatologically shaped approach to ethics may handle matters which extend beyond the boundaries of the church. I will not even attempt to articulate a comprehensive treatment of the subject. Yet our discussion will lay a bare and tentative theological groundwork for a Christian view of medical ethics which, against the "sectarian" stereotype, may properly deal with matters beyond the community of faith.

In line with an ethic of discipleship, the first step in the argument is to point to Jesus' example of physical healing in the Gospels and the ministry of healing performed by early Christians (e.g., Luke 4:31-44, 5:12-26; Acts 3:1-10). Lohfink sees Jesus' healings as eschatological "signs of the kingdom's proximity," demonstrations of the beginning of a new age of God's blessing.

> Precisely because the mighty works of Jesus were so closely connected with the inbreaking reign of God, they were also decisively concerned with the people of God. Inseparable from the eschatological horizon of Jesus' miracles is their relationship to community: they served the restoration of the people of God, among whom, in the eschatological age of salvation, no disease is permitted.[51]

Lohfink notes that Matthew and Luke portray Jesus as citing his healing of the sick as proof of his messiahship (Matt. 11:5; Luke 7:22), and that this text is an allusion to the prophetic vision of Isaiah 35:5-6:

> Then the eyes of the blind shall be opened,
>   and the ears of the deaf unstopped;
> then the lame shall leap like a deer,
>   and the tongue of the speechless sing for joy.

According to Lohfink, these Gospel narratives present Jesus in his ministry of healing as the fulfillment of Old Testament expectation, the initiator of God's reign.[52] Likewise, the apostolic healings recorded in Acts are signs of the presence of the kingdom through the power of the Spirit in the community of faith: they continue Jesus' ministry of the new age.[53]

One implication of Lohfink's account is that the Christian community, if it is to manifest a foretaste of God's kingdom, must care for those who suffer from illness even as Jesus did. Put another way, a characteristic of those who follow Jesus in kingdom ministry will be their pursuit of the physical well-being of the sick.

The same Lord who undertook such a ministry as a crucial sign of his identity is now present with the church through the Spirit as the power of the new age. So discipleship should be characterized by a reproduction of Jesus' healing praxis, mediated in a manner appropriate to present social conditions and knowledge. Hence, the church may rightly witness to the presence of God's reign through the sustenance of modern medical strategies to care for the ill.

Medical practice may be undertaken as an act of discipleship. This demonstrates, against Troeltsch and Gustafson, that the following of Jesus is not a task withdrawn from the complex physical and social realities of life, in which medicine seems always to be involved. Indeed, the Christ is not only an example of a healer but also the agent of the creation and coming redemption of all things material. Thus there is no radical discontinuity between the theologically shaped project of discipleship and the "worldly" endeavor of caring for the sick. The Christian community's establishment and support of structures which make possible care for those who suffer from illness is an action which foreshadows the blessing of God's kingdom: it is an eschatological act. Likewise, the practice of medicine by disciples formed in the community may be a proper undertaking of faithfulness to the example of the risen Lord.

Christians may pursue such a practice of medicine as a result of their formation through the disciplines of the church. This formation may help them describe their lives as opportunities for the ministry of the kingdom, in this case for the selfless service of the sick as a sign of God's new age. This sort of medical practice is a mode of resistance to the forces of sin, alienation, and death, which will be overcome by God finally in the eschaton. Such a medical practice is not only sustained by other ecclesial practices. It may well function as an activity which sustains Christians in further formation as disciples; it may lead them to other modes of resistance to evil forces by fostering certain dispositions which they did not previously possess. They may gain patience and empathy, or skills of discernment, such as the ability to be present to and serve people in great physical pain. Hence, Christians may grow as disciples through the practice of medicine.

Let us examine more explicitly the relevance of eschatology for the description of medical practice. It is helpful to consider Paul Ramsey's suggestion that a Christian view of medicine will be informed by the eschatological conviction that "there shall come a time when there will be none like us to come after us. . . . God means to kill us all in the end, and in the end He is going to succeed."[54] In this passage, Ramsey is arguing against genetic engineers who want to preclude the end of the human race through genetic deterioration by aggressive eugenic practices. In part, he attacks the logic of their proposals by exposing their assumption that it is the place of humanity to ensure its perpetuation at all costs, and that such a goal would justify any means. Ramsey responds that the Christian knows

> that he [or she] is not bound to succeed in preventing genetic deterioration, more than he [or she] would be bound to retard entropy, or prevent planets from colliding with this earth or the sun from cooling.[55]

Ramsey's comments are provocative and indicate that an eschatological description of reality may shape a view of the appropriate practice of medicine by Christians. Such practice takes place within a world destined for subordination to the Lord whom the disciple seeks to serve through acts of physical healing and care. We may weigh arguments about particular medical endeavors, such as eugenic strategies that seem to rely on Promethean illusions about the role of humanity in the universe, within the context of Christian theological claims about the nature and destiny of reality in light of the new age begun in Jesus' resurrection.

Medical ethics does not, then, concern the same problematic for all who practice medicine. Depending on the theological, philosophical, or political commitments of particular ethicists or practitioners, the description of what medical ethics is about will vary.[56]

Therefore, a basic conceptual problem for a *Christian* medical ethic is the matter of how disciples will learn what the proper practice of medicine entails in the midst of their temporal location between Pentecost and Parousia. In other words, Christians who want to imitate their Lord's ministry of healing must ask: What are the characteristics of a medical practice appropriate to location in the eschatological narrative begun in Jesus' resurrection?

One such characteristic would be the view that death is not the greatest evil or a sign of ultimate loss. Because of Jesus' resurrection, Christians believe that we will be raised up in God's fulfilled kingdom. Our deaths take place within an eschatological context that makes intelligible hope beyond death, that asks "Where, O death, is your victory? Where, O death, is your sting?" (1 Cor. 15:55). Hence, death is not a final tragedy which medicine is to resist at all costs. It is an inevitable aspect of life as we know it, an aspect which the risen Lord has conquered. We must die, but death is not the ultimate evil. This reality is conveyed in Ramsey's description of the human being as "an embodied soul or ensouled body."[57] We are mortals, fleshy creatures who must die, but death will not have the final word on our destiny or the meaning of our life.

An implication of this view of death is that Christian practitioners of medicine should allow certain dying patients to die: those whose healing is beyond the capacity of the caregiver's skill should be spared the assault of almost surely pointless treatment. Death is not so great an enemy that it must be resisted in the most exhaustive ways imaginable. Ramsey reflects such an acceptance of death in his support for a "medical indications policy" which would withdraw curative treatment when in the practitioner's judgment the treatment would simply prolong dying.[58]

When pursuing a cure is no longer an option, the practitioner's main focus in this approach will become providing palliative care for the patient, making him or her comfortable until death comes. Hence, the dying patient is not abandoned as though there is no point to medical practice when death is inevitable. On the contrary, the disciple seeks to be an instrument of

God's blessing to the dying person. Under these circumstances, the most welcome blessing is likely the relief of the patient's discomfort to as great an extent as possible.

This brief discussion of the type of treatment appropriate for dying patients presses the issue of the purpose of medicine as an act of discipleship. Since it is an endeavor that does not stop when a cure is impossible, its goal must not be limited to physical healing. Stanley Hauerwas's comments on the chronically ill are telling:

> Often we are willing to be present and sympathetic with someone with an intense but temporary pain. . . . We are willing to be present as long as they work at being "good" sick people who try to get well quickly and do not make too much of their discomfort. . . . But it seems to be asking too much of us to be compassionate year in and year out.[59]

Practitioners of medicine, however, are continually "in the presence of those who are in pain."[60] Indeed, for Hauerwas the basic task of the physician "is not to cure, but to care through being present to the one in pain."[61] In this respect, the work of the practitioner is not focused on healing as much as it is in being present to the chronically ill or dying patient. It is directed toward demonstrating that God's blessings are not only for the well. It shows that neither pain nor the prospect of death may alienate a sick person from the fellowship of the kingdom begun in Jesus' ministry and carried out now by his followers.

An implication of the commitment to be present with those who suffer from illness is that the physician will pursue a cure when that option is available. But when there is no appropriate healing strategy, the physician must be able to pursue the non-healing care of the weak, the difficult, and the hopeless patient.

The church, through its structures and procedures of moral formation, should seek to produce disciples who may undertake such a trying project of medical practice. Christians know that death and suffering are not the final word on human existence and that they must follow Jesus in a difficult journey of kingdom ministry which gives special attention to the sick and marginalized. As a result, they should be uniquely suited to this style of medical practice. Believers should learn to describe their lives as opportunities to serve God in selfless ministry to the weak even as Jesus did. In the formative community of faith, therefore, they should develop the skills to pursue a medical discipleship.[62]

Such medical concern is not, however, limited to the boundaries of the church. Christians may, for example, oppose certain society-wide medical policies on the treatment of the dying when they believe those policies wrongly underwrite a view of death as the greatest enemy. Their public critique might not be formulated exclusively in Christian theological language. Yet it is certainly an appropriate part of discipleship to advocate policies in the larger society that are in keeping with how Christians believe the dying should be treated. Through such advocacy, we pursue the ministry of the kingdom in calling for the treatment of the marginalized in a manner appropriate to our description of the world as the domain of the risen Lord.

A related aspect of a Christian medical ethic is to critique and resist structures which make medical care a privilege which the disadvantaged members of a society cannot afford and to which they are denied access. Christians are to continue Jesus' ministry of blessing the downtrodden as they practice medicine and administrate their medical institutions. They will care for persons in contemporary society who are analogous to the outcasts to whom Jesus ministered (e.g., lepers, the poor, members of scorned races, prostitutes, the demonized, and the ceremonially unclean).

By such an inclusive medical practice, Christians will demonstrate that they act in the world in accord with their description of it as the realm of the risen Lord, who demands discipleship. Hence, they will use their medical skills as tools for the ministry of God's kingdom which foreshadows a time when the lame will walk, the blind will see, and the deaf will hear. Their medical practice will be conspicuous in its attention to the needs of the marginalized, who often lack medical care.

In addition to such medical practice by Christians, disciples may call upon the larger medical, governmental, and economic structures to attend to unmet needs for medical care. Such advocacy on behalf of those who lack medical care is not part of a "Constantinian" project to compromise the gospel for the sake of sustaining a civilization. Instead, it is simply an act of discipleship, an effort by Christians to see goals pursued which are consistent with the kingdom's demands. They may use professional influence or secular political structures to achieve a just distribution of medical care. When *just* is defined in terms of what the kingdom requires, this is a proper endeavor of discipleship.[63]

This brief discussion of medical ethics has not even attempted to address the plethora of complex issues concerning the treatment of the dying and the distribution of medical care to disadvantaged groups. Nevertheless, it has served to make an important point at a basic conceptual level: Christians who pursue an eschatologically located ethic of discipleship may rightly participate in a practice of medicine that is not cloistered within the confines of the community of faith. We have seen that Christians, in light of their communal formation and theological commitments, may engage in the practice of medicine in the larger society as a proper task of the following of Jesus. Likewise, we may address medical matters in public forums, call for societal reform pursuant to our beliefs about how humans ought to relate to one another in God's world, and otherwise contribute to the life of medical institutions as we see fit.[64]

Christian participation in medical ethics, then, is an example of how our communitarian view of discipleship does not require withdrawal from the world. On the contrary, it seeks to engage the world in line with its destiny for redemption and to guide patterns of behavior which foreshadow God's fulfilled reign over the entire world. In the light of this discussion, we are justified in concluding that discipleship is not "sectarian."

5

Conclusion: Discipleship for All Believers

Our discussion thus far has shown how a particular account of eschatology may inform certain aspects of Christian moral discourse. The foundational systematic point of this project is the claim that Jesus' resurrection has begun a new age of God's kingdom which awaits its final consummation in the eschaton. Within this temporal context, Christian eschatology should be characterized fundamentally by hope in the future of the risen Lord, a hope for the coming fullness of God's reign of the sort that locates Christian existence temporally between Pentecost and Parousia. In developing this position, we have not relied primarily on a reconstructed view of apocalyptic or a reading of Jesus' preaching about the kingdom interpreted without reference to his resurrection. Instead, our discussion asks: What may we expect on the basis of Jesus' resurrection? What difference does that event and the future entailed by it make for the Christian life?

In contrast to Bultmann and Niebuhr, I maintain that this eschatology is temporal and is truly a hope for the *future*. They interpret New Testament references to a future kingdom in light of presupposed views of the static nature of reality in such a way that the Christian life is essentially viewed as atemporal, not contextualized by what is to come. Similarly, Gustafson dismisses both the resurrection of Jesus and temporal eschatological hope on the grounds of natural science. He does not regard the phenomena of the raising of the dead Jesus and the coming of a qualitatively new age to be warranted by the findings of scientific inquiry.

All these theologians find unacceptable the claim that Jesus' resurrection has a temporal significance and has begun a radically new order of God's reign which will consummate in the future subjection of all reality to God. They interpret such notions in light of assumptions about reality and history that are not shaped by, and apparently cannot take account of, the possibility that something wholly new and of unprecedented significance might occur. Indeed, their assumptions rule out the possibility that such a "history-making" or "future-making" event has taken place.

Weiss, Schweitzer, Dodd, and Wilder, in similar fashion, interpret Jesus' moral relevance primarily as a first-century moral teacher who, except in Dodd's view, was obviously mistaken in his expectations for the future. They describe Jesus' moral relevance in this way largely because it is not amenable to their historicist presuppositions to entertain the thought that someone truly novel, who does not fit within preestablished categories, might appear and even be raised from the dead. With their worldviews, they do not know how to speak of such a phenomenon as being central to the Christian life.

The point is not that they all deny that Jesus was raised from the dead, but rather that they do not see the significance of that event for the future of God's reign and, hence, for the temporal description and location of the Christian life. They settle for a view of "Jesus as moral teacher" without conveying the temporal and cosmological significance of "Jesus as risen Lord." My claim is that we must see Jesus as the risen Lord if we are to discern rightly the orientation of the Christian life as a temporally located endeavor between Pentecost and Parousia, for which that location makes a material difference.

In the first chapter I argued against such positions. The identification of Jesus as the risen Lord, whose resurrection begins the new age of God's kingdom, is an implication of the expectation created by the raising from the dead of the Jesus who was crucified as a blasphemer. The God of Israel raised Jesus after such a lowly death; that led the first Christians to believe that *he* unexpectedly was the fulfillment of Israel's hopes. Jesus transformed the very nature of those hopes; he consequently is the guarantee of God's conquest of all rebellion, sin, and death in the eschaton. Because God has overcome this most obscene spectacle of the crucifixion of the Messiah through the vindication of resurrection, Christians believe that the risen Lord will be the agent of the final subjection of all things to God.

That event of resurrection, without direct parallel in what has happened before, creates the context of its interpretation. It demands a radically new description in a way which cannot be contained by categories formulated purely in light of how humans think of what has happened previously.

Hence, these various critiqued approaches to ethics presuppose a description of reality and interpret eschatology or Jesus Christ in a way not conceptually dependent on the unique event of his resurrection. They methodologically preclude themselves from grasping "the wisdom of God" manifest in the scandal of the cross, the shock of the resurrection, and the hope of the consummated kingdom (1 Cor. 1:18-31). These scholars justify their claims by allowing extraneous hermeneutical norms to determine the theological task: assumptions about the temporal and the eternal (Bultmann, Wilder, Niebuhr), the individual and the social (Troeltsch), or the scientific and the superstitious (Gustafson). To a large extent, they control discourse about the future created in Jesus' resurrection by holding it accountable to standards that do not reckon with his resurrection being radically new. As a necessary consequence, they therefore are not able to expound adequate views of eschatology.

Our discussion works within the context of the temporal nature of the future guaranteed by the risen Lord. I have shown that the Christian life should be construed as an endeavor between Pentecost and Parousia, a temporally located reality for which that location makes a material difference. Rather than thinking about ethics in light of assumptions about the static nature of reality, I have sought to indicate what the moral life should look like in a temporal eschatological perspective which challenges other worldviews.

The second chapter demonstrated an important characteristic of my understanding of the significance of the eschatological context of Christian ethics: its ecclesial location. The church is empowered and challenged to manifest a foretaste of the kingdom through the presence of the Spirit, which is precisely the Spirit of the risen Lord. Thus ethics becomes the embodied process of discerning how to foreshadow the kingdom and how to display faithfulness in a world whose destiny lies in the future of Jesus Christ.

The community of faith should seek to pursue a communal discipleship, a socially realized faithfulness to the risen Lord, who is present in its midst since Pentecost. Believers can do this by performing practices of discipleship, sustaining communal procedures and structures that edify the church, and identifying virtues appropriate to the Christian life. In a sinful world whose corruption must be resisted, the formation of the community is essential for the production of disciples; hence, the Christian life finds its intelligibility and realization uniquely within the faith community.

In this way, our discussion is also a critique of individualistic accounts of the Christian life which do not attend to the necessity of the communal context for those who pursue fidelity to the Christ. We likewise emphasize, especially through an appropriation of the insights of Yoder and a reading of 1 Corinthians, the importance of a visible church as an identifiable social structure for Christian moral formation. Through this conceptual point on the concreteness of the church, I have displayed why ethics is not purely a theoretical matter. On the contrary, it emerges from and is nourished by the communal praxis of discipleship understood uniquely within the temporal eschatological context.

It is no wonder that theologians with nontemporal eschatologies, such as Niebuhr and Gustafson, have little concern with the church as a distinct community of central importance for the moral life. They have laid aside the belief that the coming of the Spirit at Pentecost is an eschatological event establishing the church as an eschatological community which foreshadows the future. Thus, it is easy to see how the church would cease to be of profound moral interest to them. They view the church as one of the many human communities which participate in the normal conditions of human existence; it does not have any unique identification, empowerment, or hope. In contrast with their construals, my approach holds that it is precisely the eschatological location of the church which warrants its great moral significance.

That moral significance is displayed more fully in our description of the community of faith as a social order sustaining a mode of moral discernment and description. Through that communal praxis and the work of the Spirit, Christians are enabled to pursue practical discipleship and judge what faithfulness to the risen Lord entails in particular circumstances. Within a world created by God and to be redeemed by the God incarnate in Jesus, Christians must see all reality as the domain of the risen Lord, a realm in which they learn to display discipleship. In this sense, Christians use story to understand reality and see themselves located within the temporal cosmic drama of salvation. The conclusion of that drama will be the fullness of God's reign, a discrete event to happen in the future. Within this eschatological narrative, Christians must learn to construe moral terms, such as justice, in a way that displays the requirements of discipleship. Because no aspect of the moral life is independent of the lordship of Jesus Christ, this descriptive task is extremely important.

We have also seen how an eschatological view of Christian ethics may properly attend to matters beyond the community of faith. Thus we have argued against the stereotypical view that communitarian positions which emphasize an ethic of discipleship are "sectarian" and withdrawn from the moral complexities of the world. The positions of Troeltsch and Gustafson deny the appropriateness of a view of the Christian life as discipleship and make some norm other than the following of Jesus to be the determining standard of the moral life. In contrast, we have seen that their approaches to ethics are at odds with the basic Christian assertions that the Christ is the agent of both our creation and redemption, that all reality is the domain of the God incarnate in Jesus, and that faithfulness in that realm is both possible and appropriate.

Moreover, Troeltsch and Gustafson make a theological error in evaluating understandings of the resurrection's significance as the beginning of a new age, of the church, and of the moral life: all these they hold accountable to individualistic and "scientistic" assumptions. Thus they slight the following of Jesus in the community which foreshadows God's reign; such discipleship is of marginal interest to them in comparison with the task of sustaining the dominant social order. In contrast, we view the Christian life in proper temporal perspective. Our eschatological approach makes it clear that the communal discipleship of the risen Lord simply cannot be described as marginal to God's purposes or marginal to what is ultimately true or important in history and society. Hence, our critique of Troeltsch and Gustafson is largely eschatological in nature. Their "antisectarian" argument fails to describe the Christian life in light of the radically new future begun in Jesus' resurrection, a future of which the community of faith is a part.

In chapter 4, I also explored the conceptual basis of a Christian medical ethic and showed that an eschatological approach does not require withdrawal from social orders other than the church. By asking what sort of moral analysis is appropriate to such a temporally located medical practice, we have established that the practical reason of discipleship may engage complex moral matters in contemporary society. Medicine is surely not the only extraecclesial undertaking which Christians may pursue as an act of discipleship. No aspect of God's creation is in principle ruled out as a realm in which Christians may serve the risen Lord.

Throughout this volume, I have affirmed belief in Jesus' resurrection as the beginning of a new age and described important implications of the resurrection for Christian ethics. The several chapters develop what those commitments mean for ecclesiology, the analytical tasks of ethics, and the "sectarian" debate.

The discussion indicates that eschatology may inform the discourse of Christian ethics at many levels. By attending to such topics, we have outlined important conceptual bases for an eschatologically located, communitarian discipleship ethic that is not "sectarian." I have also shown how my approach to ethics contrasts with the positions of figures such as Weiss, Schweitzer, Dodd, Bultmann, Wilder, Niebuhr, Troeltsch, and Gustafson. In examining the grounds of our disagreement, we have found that their lack of temporal eschatological convictions is a major factor in their production of problematic views of the Christian life.

This book is an invitation for believers to see the world eschatologically, to interpret and live in it as a realm destined for full redemption on account of Jesus' resurrection, and to hold other interpretations of reality accountable to that temporal expectation. Our discussion outlines a theoretical account of the church's communal manifestation of a foretaste of God's reign. It provides conceptual resources for calling the church to greater faithfulness as a distinctive community of discipleship.

My proposal is that a faithful church may sustain the practical reason of a discipleship capable of describing the moral significance of virtually any aspect of God's creation. In this way, the discussion calls for a mode of Christian ethical discourse which will guide disciples as they seek to follow their Lord in the ministry of the kingdom in the midst of a rebellious world. That world, and the entirety of the moral life, should be described in light of the new age begun in the resurrection of Jesus Christ.

Precisely what such moral description will entail and require is a matter to be worked out by particular faith communities in their specific situations. Since I am calling for an eschatologically located *practical* reason of discipleship, this position requires a discernment that is sensitive to the diverse circumstances in which Christians will pursue faithfulness to their Lord. What is crucial is that their pursuit of discipleship be construed as a communally sustained endeavor to be faithful to the Christ in whose future lies the destiny of all reality. This eschatological context should shape and inform the Christian life in determinate ways because eschatology is of central importance for Christian ethics.

Notes

Chapter 1
Jesus' Resurrection As the Beginning of a New Age

1. I use the term *new age* to express the significance of Jesus' resurrection for several reasons. First, I think it conveys well Paul's sense of a qualitatively new time of grace, righteousness, life, and resurrection that has been initiated by the risen Lord (Rom. 5:12-21; 1 Cor. 15:20-28). As "Christ is the end of the law so that there may be righteousness for everyone who believes," Gentiles are now "grafted in" to the salvation of the God of Israel (Rom. 10:4; 11:17). Likewise, Christ is the fulfillment of Jeremiah's hope for the time of "a new covenant" (Jer. 31:31-34; Heb. 8:8-13). The term *new age* also points to the new presence of God's Spirit that created the church at Pentecost only after the resurrection (Acts 2:33). The resurrection of Jesus begins the end of "the present evil age" (Gal. 1:4), which one day will give way to "a new heaven and a new earth" (Rev. 21:1). That consummated order is the final fulfillment of Jesus' preaching that "the kingdom of God has come near" or "is at hand" (Mark 1:15).

My use of the term *new age* should not be confused with the current faddish use of *New Age*, which in some quarters refers to a spirituality founded upon a mixture of popular psychology and a selective interpretation of Eastern religious traditions. In contrast to the so-called New Age Movement, my use of *new age* is explicitly biblical in derivation. I use the term to display the import of theological convictions which are central to historic Christianity.

2. By the term *temporally located*, I mean location within a sequence of events in time as opposed to *static* or *timeless*. Throughout the book, *temporal eschatology* or *temporal hope* signifies the location of the Christian life between the sequential events of Pentecost and Parousia in a way that indicates a futuristic aspect of hope for the fullness of God's kingdom. The consummation of God's reign is an event to occur in the future. We live after the events of Jesus' resurrection and the coming of the Spirit at Pentecost and before the Parousia (the second coming of Christ). I intend nothing more by the use of *temporal* than this point of location within a sequence of events.

3. Albrecht Ritschl, *The Christian Doctrine of Justification and Reconciliation* (Clifton, N.J.: Reference Book Publishers, 1966), 284. I am indebted to the first four essays in *The Kingdom of God in 20th-Century Interpretation*, ed. by Wendell Willis (Peabody, Mass.: Hendrickson Publishers, 1987), for describing lucidly the development of biblical scholarship on ethics and eschatology since the end of the nineteenth century. The treatments of a number of issues in these essays have helped me research and think through the following account of biblical studies and ethics.

4. Johannes Weiss, *Jesus' Proclamation of the Kingdom of God* (Philadelphia: Fortress Press, 1971), 114, 132.

5. Ibid., 131.

6. Ibid., 135.

7. Ibid., 134.

8. Albert Schweitzer, *The Quest for the Historical Jesus* (New York: Macmillan Company, 1968), 367.

9. Ibid., 380ff.

10. Schweitzer, *Civilization and Ethics* (London: A & C Black Ltd., 1923), 71.

11. Ibid., 72.

12. Ibid., 251.

13. Richard H. Hiers, Jr., "Pivotal Reactions to the Eschatological Interpretations: Rudolf Bultmann and C. H. Dodd," in *The Kingdom of God in 20th-Century Interpretation*, 16-17.

14. C. H. Dodd, *The Parables of the Kingdom* (New York: Charles Scribner's Sons, 1961), 82.

15. Ibid., 28-31. See also Hiers, 18ff.

16. Dodd, *The Apostolic Preaching and Its Developments* (London: Hodder and Stoughton, 1936), 21ff.

17. Hiers, 23.

18. Dodd, *Gospel and Law: The Relation of Faith and Ethics in Early Christianity* (New York: Columbia University Press, 1951), 62.

19. Ibid., 45.

20. Rudolf Bultmann, *Jesus Christ and Mythology* (New York: Charles Scribner's Sons, 1951), 12. For a concise, lucid description of Bultmann's eschatology within the context of his larger theological project, see Raul Gabas Pallas, *Escatologia protestante in la actualidad* (Vitoriensa: Publicationes del Seminario de Vitoria [Spain], vol. 20), 1964:201-229. See also Hiers, 24ff.

21. Bultmann, *Jesus Christ and Mythology*, 22.

22. Bultmann, *Jesus and the Word* (New York: Charles Scribner's Sons, 1958), 131.

23. Bultmann, *Existence and Faith* (New York: Meridian Books, 1960), 186.

24. Bultmann, *Jesus and the Word*, 40-41.

25. Hiers, 26.

26. Bultmann, "The Study of the Synoptic Gospels," *Form Criticism*, ed., F. C. Grant (New York: Harper & Row Publishers, 1962), 73; Bultmann, *Jesus and the Word*, 127-128.

27. Bultmann, *Jesus and the Word*, 117-118, 79.

28. Bultmann, *Theology of the New Testament*, vol.1 (New York: Charles Scribner's Sons, 1951), 15.

29. Bultmann, *Jesus and the Word*, 48.

30. Bultmann, "New Testament and Mythology," in *Kergyma and Myth*, ed. by H. W. Bartsch (New York: Harper and Row Publishers, 1961), 5. See also John Macquarrie, "Rudolf Bultmann," in *A Handbook of Christian Theologians*, ed. by Dean Peerman and Martin Marty (Nashville: Abingdon Press, 1984), 447ff.

31. See Jürgen Moltmann's reading of Bultmann on this point: Moltmann, *Theology of Hope: On the Ground and the Implications of a Christian Eschatology* (New York: Harper & Row Publishers, 1967), 58ff.

32. Amos Wilder, *Eschatology and Ethics in the Teaching of Jesus* (New York: Harper & Brothers Publishers, 1939), 237.

33. Ibid., 153-155.

34. Ibid., 161.

35. Ibid., 193.

36. Ibid., 195-197.

37. Ibid., 232.

38. Ibid., 231.

39. Ibid., 199.

40. Ibid., 162ff., 242ff.

41. Norman Perrin, *The Kingdom of God in the Teaching of Jesus* (London: SCM Press, 1963), 159. See also Oscar Cullmann, *Christ and Time* (Philadelphia: Westminster Press, 1950), 84, 144ff., for an account of God's reign as both present and future.

42. Perrin, 164.

43. Ibid., 167.

44. Ibid., 184.

45. John Collins cites this definition in his *The Apocalyptic Imagination* (New York: Crossroad Books, 1984), 4.

46. Ibid., 205, 207.

47. J. Christiaan Beker, *Paul the Apostle* (Philadelphia: Fortress Press, 1980), 135-136.

48. Ibid., 147.

49. Ibid., 152.

50. Rolf Rendtorff, "The Concept of Revelation in Ancient Israel," in *Revelation as History*, ed. by Wolfhart Pannenberg (New York: The Macmillan Company, 1965), 37.

51. Moltmann, 16-17.

52. Ibid., 192-194.

53. Ibid., 191-192.

54. Ibid., 192-193.

55. Ibid., 194.

56. Ibid., 198.

57. Ibid., 201. While Moltmann's way of making this point reflects the influence of Hegel upon him, one does not have to be a Hegelian to appreciate the temporal thrust of Paul's "first fruits" language (1 Cor. 15:20-28) or the irony of the God of Israel raising "this Jesus whom you crucified" (Acts 2:36). See Christopher Morse, *The Logic of Promise in Moltmann's Theology* (Philadelphia: Fortress Press, 1979), 12-15, for a discussion of Hegel and Bloch's influence on both Moltmann and Pannenberg.

58. Thomas N. Finger, *Christian Theology: An Eschatological Approach*, vol. 1 (Scottdale, Pa.: Herald Press, 1985), 351-352.

59. Ibid., 350ff.

60. Wolfhart Pannenberg, *Jesus—God and Man* (Philadelphia: The Westminster Press, 1977), 67-68. The high priest heard blasphemy in Jesus' claim to be the coming exalted judge (Matt. 26:64). A claim to be the Messiah was not blasphemous.

61. Ibid., 67.

62. Ibid., 69.

63. Ibid., 367.

64. Ibid., 83.

65. Ibid., 81.

66. Walter Kasper, *Jesus the Christ* (New York: Paulist Press, 1976), 154-155.

67. Ibid., 155.

68. While Christian eschatology is controlled primarily by christological convictions, it remains helpful to use *eschatology* as a distinct theological term to designate inquiry into expectation for the fulfillment of reality in the eschaton. As this consummation entails the Son's subjection to the Father, and is hence a Trinitarian event, it is important not to collapse eschatology entirely into Christology (1 Cor. 15:24-28).

69. Jon Sobrino, *Christology at the Crossroads* (Maryknoll, New York: Orbis Books, 1978), 242.

70. Ibid., 243.

71. See Bruce Metzger, *The New Testament, Its Background, Growth, and Content* (Nashville: Abingdon Press, 1983), 150-151, for a discussion of the peculiarity of Jesus' messiahship within the context of first-century Israel. See Mark 8:27-33, John 5:1-18, and Matthew 11:19 for passages from the Gospels that portray the uniqueness of Jesus' ministry.

72. I am not suggesting that these theologians have identical eschatologies or that they formulate the significance of Jesus' resurrection for the future in precisely the same way. I refer to them, rather, because they insist that a view of Jesus' resurrection as the beginning of a new age, as the guarantee of the future of God's reign, is a central aspect of Christian belief.

73. Pentecost presupposes the resurrection because God's sending of the Spirit to the church of Jesus Christ makes sense only as an action that continues God's presence with the followers of the risen and ascended Lord. Were it not for Jesus' resurrection, the disciples would likely have gone their separate ways and "Pentecost" would simply be the Greek name for the Jewish Feast of Weeks (Luke 24:21).

74. French L. Arrington, *Paul's Aeon Theology in 1 Corinthians* (Washington, D.C.: University Press of America, 1978), 135.

75. Gerhard Lohfink, *Jesus and Community* (Philadelphia: Fortress Press, 1984), 82. Lohfink emphasizes the continuity of Jewish expectation with Jesus' ministry and resurrection, and uses *eschatology* as a term to describe the matrix of hope which Christians believe Jesus has fulfilled. As such, he is not so much participating in the historical-critical debate on "apocalyptic" as he is attempting to make the theological case that Jesus' significance may not be discerned rightly apart from explicit reference to the faith of Israel as that is reflected in the Old Testament.

76. Ibid., 85.

77. Ibid., 86.

78. Carl E. Braaten, *The Future of God* (New York: Harper & Row Publishers, 1969), 120.

79. Moltmann, 174.

80. Ibid., 175-177.

81. Ibid., 177.

82. My point is not that these theologians reject the claim that Jesus was raised from death by God, but that they do not incorporate his identity as the risen Lord, in whose future lies the destiny of all reality for subjection to God, in a determining or central way in their approaches to Christian ethics. At least for the purpose of describing Jesus' moral significance, they attend to him primarily

as "teacher," not as the risen Lord. Hence, their eschatologies lack the temporal orientation which is grounded in God's victory through Jesus over death. They fail to see how the resurrection has begun a new age in which we live between Pentecost and Parousia.

83. Ibid., 180-181.

84. Schweitzer, *The Quest for the Historical Jesus*, 399.

85. Certainly the existence of the New Testament and the founding of the Christian church are dependent in a historical sense on belief in Jesus' resurrection. Were it not for that belief, the social movement called Christianity would not have come about. Likewise, the identification of Jesus as the Christ or Son of God is an implication of the belief that God has uniquely vindicated Jesus through resurrection.

86. Weiss, 135.

87. Ibid., 134.

88. Bultmann, *Jesus and the Word*, 40-41; Wilder, 153-155.

89. Bultmann, *Jesus and the Word*, 131.

90. Hiers, 29, for example, comments that for Bultmann "ethics is conceptualized entirely in terms of self-centered self-actualization; the neighbor drops out of sight."

91. Ibid., 31.

Chapter 2:
Church As Proleptic Social Locus of the New Age

1. By *church* I mean any group of Christians which seeks as a group to be faithful to the risen Lord. In this chapter, I am attempting to provide conceptual insight on what the faithfulness of any such group would entail, on how groups of Christians may begin the arduous task of discerning what it means for them to be faithful in a given situation. Rather than providing a detailed analysis of what the faithfulness of a particular group in a particular setting would involve, I describe basic aspects of the theological logic that makes the notion of church intelligible. In that light, I invite particular churches to pursue faithfulness in a manner appropriate to their given situations and challenges. I use the term *community* in the same sense as church. *Eschatological community* refers to the church's identity as a foretaste of the new age begun in Jesus' resurrection through the power of the Spirit.

Examples of the sorts of communities which I have foremost in mind in this chapter are these: congregations which seek to nurture their members in certain modes of resistance to the dominant cultural order in light of the gospel; Latin American base communities; and organizations such as the Baptist Peace Fellowship of North America, Evangelicals for Social Action, and Bread for the World, which assist congregations in sustaining discipleship. The common trait of such communities is that they seek to pursue faithfulness to Jesus Christ through a critical, self-conscious relationship with the larger society in which they find themselves. See, for example, Phillip Berryman, *Liberation Theology* (New York: Pantheon Books, 1987), 63-79; Gil Dawes, "Working People and the Church: Profile of a Liberated Church in Reactionary Territory," in *Churches in Struggle*, ed. by William K. Tabb (New York: Monthly Review Press, 1986), 223-239; Arthur Simon, *Bread for the World* (New York: Paulist Press, 1975); Frederick Herzog, *Justice Church* (Maryknoll, New York: Orbis Books, 1980); Stanley

Hauerwas, *Christian Existence Today* (Durham, N.C.: The Labyrinth Press, 1988), 111-131.

2. See my dissertation, *The Import of Eschatology in John Howard Yoder's Critique of Constantinianism* (San Francisco: Mellen Research University Press, 1992), for a critical assessment of Yoder's approach to Christian social ethics and an exhaustive listing of Yoder's publications. While the conclusions of the dissertation are critical of Yoder in many respects, I continue to think that he frames well the basic challenge of the church to be a foretaste of the new age. Hence, it is fitting to engage him constructively in this context.

3. John Howard Yoder, *The Priestly Kingdom* (Notre Dame: University of Notre Dame Press, 1984), 92.

4. Yoder, *The Politics of Jesus* (Grand Rapids, Michigan: Eerdmans Publishing Company, 1972), 11, 23.

5. Yoder, *The Priestly Kingdom*, 11.

6. Michel Foucault, "Truth and Power," in *The Foucault Reader*, ed. Paul Rabinow (New York: Pantheon Books, 1984), 59.

7. Ibid., 72-74.

8. As a Christian theologian, I reject this antitheological aspect of Foucault's project, for God is not simply a social construct. I nevertheless want to appropriate critically Foucault's antitheoretical position in order to advance my view of the Christian life as a socially realized undertaking. Such a use of Foucault is controversial, for if I were to accept Foucault's method in its entirety, the sort of confessional theology that I am pursuing in this book would be impossible. I want to make clear, therefore, that I am consciously marshaling Foucault for the service of a theological project of which he would certainly not approve.

9. Foucault, 72-73.

10. Yoder, *The Priestly Kingdom*, 7.

11. Ibid., 35-38.

12. Yoder, *The Politics of Jesus*, 107-108.

13. Ibid., 108.

14. Yoder, *The Christian Witness to the State* (Newton, Kansas: Faith and Life Press, 1964), 13.

15. Ibid., 13, 17.

16. Ibid., 18.

17. Ibid., 19-20.

18. Ibid., 20.

19. Yoder, *The Priestly Kingdom*, 27.

20. Ibid., 27-28.

21. Ibid., 29.

22. Ibid., 31.

23. Ibid., 32-33.

24. Ibid., 33.

25. Ibid., 34.

26. Ibid., 35.

27. Ibid., 36.

28. Ibid., 37.

29. Ibid., 45.

30. Hendrik Berkhof, *Christ and the Powers* (Scottdale, Pennsylvania: Herald Press, 1962), 30.

31. Ibid., 51.

32. By *practices*, I mean nothing more than human behaviors that for contingent reasons are discerned to be significant for the sustenance of a social structure or the pursuit of moral formation. Such practices, within the context of our discussion, are modes of resistance to a dominant cultural order characterized by sin. The particulars of how practices interrelate in given situations, and how that interrelation shapes moral development, is a matter that may be addressed properly only by particular faith communities in the midst of their pursuit of faithfulness. In this sense, precise judgment on the interrelation of practices is a matter of practical reason for which the particulars of a given context are of great importance. See, for example, Jim Wallis, ed., *Waging Peace: A Handbook for the Struggle to Abolish Nuclear Weapons* (San Francisco: Harper & Row Publishers, 1982); Ronald J. Sider, *Rich Christians in an Age of Hunger: A Biblical Study* (Downers Grove, Ill.: InterVarsity Press, 1977); James H. Cone, *For My People: Black Theology and the Black Church* (Maryknoll, N.Y.: Orbis Books, 1984); and Richard J. Foster, *Freedom of Simplicity* (San Francisco: Harper & Row Publishers, 1981) for particular accounts of how Christians, facing different challenges in different situations, have called for resistance to the dominant order as an act or practice of discipleship.

33. Many who take the Supper likely do not think of its significance in this way. Yet the example of Jesus' pursuit of kingdom ministry in a fashion that led to his death coupled with his call to "take up your cross and follow me" indicates that the imitation of Christ may lead any Christian to his or her death, even as countless Christians have followed him in martyrdom whether at the hands of the Roman Empire or the El Salvadoran military.

34. James McClendon, *Ethics: Systematic Theology*, vol. 1 (Nashville: Abingdon Press, 1986), 255-259.

35. Augustine, *The City of God* (New York: Random House, Inc., 1950), 1.35 (38).

36. Bryan Turner, *Religion and Social Theory: A Materialist Perspective* (London: Heinemann Educational Books, 1983), 225. I am using the sociological "text" presented by Turner as a reading of how religion functions in contemporary society in order to portray more clearly the social conditions which the church faces in, among other places, North America.

37. Ibid., 239-40.

38. Ibid., 240-241.

39. Of course, Turner's analysis could be taken to the extreme point of suggesting that no alternative moral formation is possible under present conditions, due to the powerful forces of regulation in society. That conclusion is unwarranted, however, because of the example of Christians who resist, more or less successfully, the dominant social forces. I think here of members of religious orders; people who serve in voluntary capacities in the service of the poor, whether with the Mennonite Central Committee, the Catholic Worker movement, or other groups; Christians involved in political action groups such as Evangelicals for Social Action, Bread for the World, and the Baptist Peace Fellowship of North America; congregations that seek to sustain their members in various modes of discipleship; and resistant Christian communes like Jonah House, as described by Philip Berrigan and Elizabeth McAlister in *The Time's Discipline: The Beatitudes and Nuclear Resistance* (Baltimore, Maryland: Fortkamp Publishing Company, 1989).

40. James Cone, *God of the Oppressed* (New York: Seabury Press, 1975), 2-3.

41. Pierre Bourdieu provides an interesting sociological analysis of the role of structures and forces in the production of "cultural needs," desires, and preferences in French society. His analysis, in addition to that of Turner, leads me to place great weight on the importance of the social formation of the individual. As with Turner, I am incorporating the social scientific discourse of Bourdieu into my theological project as a reading of how society functions that sheds light on the practical, social nature of moral formation under present conditions. See Pierre Bourdieu, *Distinction: A Social Critique of the Judgement of Taste* (Cambridge, Mass.: Harvard University Press, 1984), 1.

42. Robert E. Webber and Rodney Clapp, *People of the Truth: The Power of the Worshipping Community in the Modern World* (San Francisco: Harper & Row Publishers, 1988), 55.

43. Ibid., 56.

44. Ibid., 59.

45. Ibid., 60.

46. Ibid., 63.

47. Ibid., 65.

48. Ibid., 67.

49. See Gal. 5:22.

50. French L. Arrington, *Paul's Aeon Theology in 1 Corinthians* (Washington, D.C.: University Press of America, 1978), 135.

51. Donald P. McNeill, Douglas A. Morrison, and Henri J. M. Nouwen, for example, emphasize the importance of compassion as an eschatologically located virtue: "In fact, we can only live the compassionate life to the fullest when we know that it points beyond itself. . . . Although we are still waiting in expectation, the first signs of the new earth and the new heaven, which have been promised to us and for which we hope, are already visible in the community of faith where the compassionate God reveals himself. This is the foundation of our faith, the basis of our hope, and the source of our love." McNeill, Morrison, and Nouwen, *Compassion: A Reflection on the Christian Life* (Garden City, N.Y.: Doubleday & Company, Inc., 1982), 134-135.

52. Ernst Käsemann, *New Testament Questions of Today* (Philadelphia: Fortress Press, 1969), 126.

53. Ibid., 126, 135.

Chapter 3
Moral Discussion and Practical Reason
in Eschatological Context

1. I understand moral descriptions, such as "she is just" or "that relationship is an instance of adultery," to be made as a result of the observed presence of characteristics that are indicative or constitutive of the manifestation of a quality like justice or an action like the performance of adultery. The characteristics that justify those descriptions are produced out of the substantive moral commitments of the speaker: the descriptive term embodies those commitments. Hence, so long as we know something of what the speaker means by using terms like *justice* or *adultery*, we do not have to ask whether justice is good or adultery is bad. A judgment, a profound moral position, is implicit in the use of the descriptive term. In this sense, the use of moral terms may be understood as an endeavor in description. See Julius Kovesi, *Moral Notions* (London: Rout-

ledge and Kegan Paul, 1967); and Charles Pinches, "Describing Morally: An Inquiry Concerning the Role of Description in Christian Ethics" (Ph.D. diss., University of Notre Dame, 1984), 111-162, for lucid accounts of moral description.

2. See Alasdair MacIntyre's treatment of competing views of justice in his *After Virtue* (Notre Dame: University of Notre Dame Press, 1984), 244-245.

3. Ibid., 208.

4. Ibid., 210.

5. Ibid., 209-211.

6. I think that MacIntyre's analysis of narrative nicely illuminates the temporal nature of Christian eschatological expectation. Yet I do not view his argument as an autonomous philosophical foundation necessary to legitimate a fundamentally theological hope for the future. On the contrary, his view of the significance of a narrative context for the description of human action is a philosophical position which may be incorporated critically by Christian theology in order to advance its pursuit of *theological* clarity.

Hence, I am suggesting neither that the acceptance of MacIntyre's view of narrative requires an acceptance of my view of eschatology, nor that the construction of acceptable views of God's kingdom requires reference to MacIntyre. What I am arguing is that his position on narrative may be employed to facilitate the display of the temporal nature of Christian eschatological convictions. In this sense, I am not equating narrative and eschatology, but am rather insisting that sufficient points of commonality exist between the two notions to warrant the use of the term *narrative* as a way of indicating the temporal nature of eschatology. It is to such a reading that I refer when I speak of the world as a storied realm destined for final redemption.

I use the term *storied* purely in this narrative sense, and not in the hierarchical sense of a three-storied universe or a two-storied building.

7. John Howard Yoder, "Armaments and Eschatology," *Studies in Christian Ethics*, vol. 1, no. 1 (Edinburgh: T. & T. Clark Publishers, 1988), 53.

8. Ibid., 53-58.

9. MacIntyre, *Whose Justice? Which Rationality?* (Notre Dame: University of Notre Dame Press, 1988), 339.

10. Ibid., 341; MacIntyre, *After Virtue*, 162.

11. John Howard Yoder, *The Priestly Kingdom* (Notre Dame: University of Notre Dame Press, 1984), 37. See my dissertation, *The Import of Eschatology in John Howard Yoder's Critique of Constantinianism* (San Francisco: Mellen Research University Press, 1992), chapters 2 and 4, for a critical account of Yoder's view of Jesus' moral relevance.

12. Yoder, *The Priestly Kingdom*, 75.

13. Ibid., 76; cf. John Howard Yoder, *When War Is Unjust: Being Honest in Just-War Thinking* (Minneapolis: Augsburg Fortress, 1984); and *Nevertheless: The Varieties and Shortcomings of Religious Pacifism*, 3d ed. (Scottdale, Pa.: Herald Press, 1992).

14. See Jon Sobrino, *Christology at the Crossroads* (Maryknoll, N.Y.: Orbis Books, 1978), 388-395, for a brief discussion of discipleship which appropriately takes "account of the differences between Jesus' own situation and that of present-day Christians."

15. Yoder, *The Priestly Kingdom*, 92.

16. Ibid., 92-93.

17. Ibid., 118.

18. Reinhold Niebuhr, *Reinhold Niebuhr on Politics*, eds., Harry R. Davis

and Robert C. Good (New York: Charles Scribner's Sons, 1960), 131-133.

19. Niebuhr, *An Interpretation of Christian Ethics* (New York: The Seabury Press, 1979), 23-28.

20. Niebuhr, *Reinhold Niebuhr on Politics*, 135-136.

21. Niebuhr, *An Interpretation of Christian Ethics*, 116.

22. Duane K. Friesen, *Christian Peacemaking and International Conflict* (Scottdale, Pa.: Herald Press, 1986), 98.

23. Ibid., 98-99.

24. Niebuhr, *The Nature and Destiny of Man*, vol. 2 (New York: Charles Scribner's Sons, 1943), 289.

25. Niebuhr, *The Nature and Destiny of Man*, vol. 1 (New York: Charles Scribner's Sons, 1941), 17.

26. Niebuhr, *An Interpretation of Christian Ethics*, 35-36.

27. Ibid., 55.

28. Dennis P. McCann, *Christian Realism and Liberation Theology* (Maryknoll, New York: Orbis Books, 1981), 87-103.

29. Niebuhr, *An Interpretation of Christian Ethics*, 69.

30. Ibid., 64, 85.

31. Yoder, *The Politics of Jesus*, 132.

32. Ibid., 240-250.

33. Yoder, *The Christian Witness to the State* (Newton, Kansas: Faith and Life Press, 1964), 49.

34. McCann, 82-87.

35. While Niebuhr locates the individual moral agent within the larger context of the dominant institutions of society, his view of Christian ethics is individualistic in the sense of having no significant moral role for the church or for any Christian social entity larger than the individual.

36. MacIntyre, *Whose Justice? Which Rationality?*, 389.

37. L. Gregory Jones, "Should Christians Affirm Rawls's Justice as Fairness? A Response to Professor Beckley," *The Journal of Religious Ethics* 16 (Fall 1988): 268.

38. Ibid., 168.

39. Ibid., p. 266.

40. John Rawls, *A Theory of Justice* (Cambridge: Belknap Press of Harvard University, 1971); Michael Walzer, *Spheres of Justice* (New York: Basic Books, 1983).

41. MacIntyre, *After Virtue*, 270.

42. Friesen, 112.

43. Ibid., 113-114.

44. Ibid., 115-117.

45. Ibid., 117-122.

46. Ibid., 80-101.

Chapter 4
Is Discipleship "Sectarian"?

1. See, for example, H. Richard Niebuhr's discussion of the "Christ Against Culture" paradigm in his *Christ and Culture* (New York: Harper & Row Publishers, 1951), 45-82; and Reinhold Niebuhr's treatment of "The Ethic of Jesus" in *An Interpretation of Christian Ethics* (New York: The Seabury Press,

1979), 22-38. Each portrays an ethic of discipleship in a fashion that makes it an inappropriate model for guiding Christian social involvement.

2. Ernst Troeltsch, *The Social Teachings of the Christian Churches* (New York: The MacMillan Company, 1931), 32, 379-80, 1000, 1011.

3. Friesen, "Normative Factors in Troeltsch's Typology of Religious Association," *Journal of Religious Ethics* 3 (Fall 1975): 273.

4. Ibid., 274.

5. Troeltsch, 52.

6. Ibid., 999.

7. Friesen, "Normative Factors in Troeltsch's Typology of Religious Association," 277.

8. Ibid., 279; I am not comfortable with Friesen's description of Luther as a mystic and think that it is more helpful simply to see a significant polarity in Luther's ethical reflections between the direct relevance of faith and love for the individual and the "worldly" requirements of social responsibility. See Martin Luther's "Secular Authority: To What Extent It Should Be Obeyed," *Martin Luther: Selections From His Writings*, ed. John Dillenberger (Garden City, N.Y.: Anchor Books, 1961), 363-402.

9. Friesen, "Normative Factors in Troeltsch's Typology of Religious Association," 271.

10. While Troeltsch was a historian who attended explicitly to the social contexts in which ideas were produced, his theological commitments display a reliance on an essentially individualistic view of Christian faith. Troeltsch, 52. Though Troeltsch had an obvious interest in the social relevance of the faith, our analysis has shown that his approach to the Christian life wrongly distorted the task of communal discipleship for the sake of underwriting an ethic of compromise with the dominant institutions of society.

11. John Howard Yoder, *The Christian Witness to the State* (Newton, Kan.: Faith and Life Press, 1964), 8-22; *The Priestly Kingdom* (Notre Dame: University of Notre Dame Press, 1984), 80-101.

12. Yoder, *The Priestly Kingdom*, 136-137. See my work on *The Import of Eschatology in John Howard Yoder's Critique of Constantinianism* (San Francisco: Mellen Research University Press, 1992), chapter 3, for an extended analysis of Yoder's argument against Constantinianism. As that chapter indicates, Yoder's account of Constantinianism is weak at a number of points, especially in his failure to display in exacting historical detail precisely how Constantinianism has been a pervasive perversion of Christian ethics since the fourth century.

Nevertheless, Yoder's use of the term *Constantinianism* retains great rhetorical force for identifying the following errors in Christian moral reasoning: (1) compromising the demands of the gospel in order for the church to gain worldly power and prestige; (2) "baptizing" uncritically a dominant cultural order which is in tension with the exigencies of God's reign; and (3) seeing the church as just another form of human social organization with no peculiar moral identity, as not being a foretaste of the new age and distinct from the larger society. My use of the term "Constantinian" in the following pages is simply a shorthand way of indicating the presence of these errors. Likewise, I place *Christian* in quotation marks, as in "Christian" empire, to indicate the use of the adjective in a nominal or "Constantinian" way.

13. Certainly Troeltsch uses *sectarian* in this way; his major reason for distinguishing sects from churches is that the former simply cannot sustain a civilization and do not participate in and contribute adequately to larger social structures. Troeltsch, 32, 379-380, 1000, 1011.

14. Yoder, *The Priestly Kingdom*, 137.

15. Yoder, "A People in the World: Theological Interpretation," *The Concept of the Believers' Church*, ed. James Leo Garrett (Scottdale, Pa.: Herald Press, 1969), 256-257.

16. Ibid., 259.

17. Ibid., 259, 276-277.

18. Ibid., 264.

19. Ibid., 265-271.

20. James Gustafson, "The Sectarian Temptation: Reflections on Theology, the Church, and the University," *Proceedings of the Catholic Theological Society* 40 (1985): 90-91.

21. Ibid., 93.

22. Ibid., 92.

23. Ibid., 93.

24. Ibid., 94.

25. Ibid., 92.

26. *Bioethics and the Beginning of Life: An Anabaptist Perspective*, eds. Roman J. Miller and Beryl H. Brubaker (Scottdale, Pa.: Herald Press, 1990), contains a number of essays on bioethical issues which are written by Christians with expertise in the natural sciences, medicine, the social sciences, and jurisprudence, as well as essays by theologians and biblical scholars. The volume is a good example of how Christians may incorporate critically various sources of "worldly wisdom" for the sake of illuminating the demands of discipleship in the contemporary world.

27. Ibid., 94; Gustafson, *Ethics from a Theocentric Perspective*, vol. 1 (Chicago: The University of Chicago, 1981) 146-154, 178-187.

28. Gustafson, *Ethics from a Theocentric Perspective*, 1:178.

29. Ibid., 264.

30. Ibid., 276.

31. Ibid., 316.

32. Ibid., 327-328.

33. Ibid., 276.

34. Gustafson, *Christ and the Moral Life* (New York: Harper & Row Publishers, 1968), 238-271.

35. Gustafson, *Ethics from a Theocentric Perspective*, 1:275-277.

36. Gustafson, "The Sectarian Temptation: Reflections on Theology, the Church, and the University," 93.

37. Gustafson, *Ethics from a Theocentric Perspective*, 1:268.

38. Gustafson, *Ethics from a Theocentric Perspective*, 1:327.

39. Ibid., 270-272.

40. Gustafson, *Ethics from a Theocentric Perspective*, vol. 2 (Chicago: The University of Chicago, 1984), 98.

41. Rom. 1:4; 1 Cor. 15:20-28; Acts 2:17-21.

42. Gustafson, *Ethics from a Theocentric Perspective*, 1:327-328.

43. Gustafson, "Moral Discernment in the Christian Life," *Norm and Context in Christian Ethics*, eds. Gene H. Outka and Paul Ramsey (New York: Charles Scribner's Sons, 1968), 31.

44. Gustafson, *Ethics from a Theocentric Perspective*, 2:302.

45. Ibid., 319.

46. Gustafson, *Ethics from a Theocentric Perspective*, 1:264.

47. Gustafson, "The Sectarian Temptation: Reflections on Theology, the Church, and the University," 93; Yoder, *The Priestly Kingdom*, 136-137.

48. Gustafson, "The Sectarian Temptation: Reflections on Theology, the Church, and the University," 93.

49. Yoder, *The Priestly Kingdom*, 137.

50. Ibid., 136-137.

51. Gerhard Lohfink, *Jesus and Community* (Philadelphia: Fortress Press, 1984), 12-13.

52. Ibid., 13-14.

53. Ibid., 81-87.

54. Paul Ramsey, *Fabricated Man: The Ethics of Genetic Control* (New Haven: Yale University Press, 1970), 25-27.

55. Ibid., 29.

56. This point harks back to MacIntyre's emphasis on the importance of the identity of the agent of practical reason for the description of a moral project. See MacIntyre, *Whose Justice? Which Rationality?* (Notre Dame: University of Notre Dame Press, 1988), 339. To see the force of this point for medicine, compare, for example, the different descriptions of medical ethics by Leon Kass in *Toward a More Natural Science* (New York: The Free Press, 1985); Edmund Pellegrino and David Thomasma in *A Philosophical Basis of Medical Practice* (New York: Oxford University Press, 1981); and Tom Beauchamp and James Childress in *Principles of Biomedical Ethics* (New York: Oxford Press, 1983).

57. Paul Ramsey, *The Patient as Person* (New Haven: Yale University Press 1970), xiii.

58. Paul Ramsey, *Ethics at the Edges of LIfe*, (New Haven: Yale University Press, 1978), 177.

59. Stanley Hauerwas, *Suffering Presence* (Notre Dame: University of Notre Dame Press, 1986), 77.

60. Ibid., 78.

61. Ibid., 79.

62. I am not suggesting, however, that Christians alone have the resources to sustain a selfless medical practice. My point is that there are resources in the Christian tradition that are especially suited to giving rise to such a practice of medicine. Certainly, Christians should rejoice when people of other traditions practice medicine in ways that are consistent with their theologically shaped view of health care.

63. Ronald J. Sider and A. Stephen Barr, writing in the organ of Evangelicals for Social Action, "Should the Poor Have Health Care?" *ESA Advocate*, January/February 1990:1-4, call for this sort of justice in their claim that the lack of health insurance by thirty-seven million people in the United States is "an affront to the God of justice. . . . This national scandal blatantly violates God's mandate to care for the sick in our midst. It must—and can—be corrected."

64. I take Hauerwas's testimony before the Ethics Advisory Board of the Department of Health, Education, and Welfare on *in vitro* fertilization to be an example of such involvement. Hauerwas, *Suffering Presence*, 142-156.

Bibliography of Works Cited

Arrington, French L. *Paul's Aeon Theology in 1 Corinthians.* Washington, D.C.: University Press of America, 1978.

Augustine, *The City of God.* New York: Random House, Inc., 1950.

Bartsch, H. W., ed. *Kerygma and Myth.* New York: Harper & Row Publishers, 1961.

Beauchamp, Tom, and James Childress. *Principles of Biomedical Ethics.* New York: Oxford University Press, 1983.

Beker, J. Christiaan. *Paul the Apostle.* Philadelphia: Fortress Press, 1980.

Berkhof, Hendrik. *Christ and the Powers.* Scottdale, Pa.: Herald Press, 1962.

Berrigan, Philip, and Elizabeth McAlister. *The Time's Discipline: The Beatitudes and Nuclear Resistance.* Baltimore, Md.: Fortkamp Publishing Company, 1989.

Berryman, Phillip. *Liberation Theology.* New York: Pantheon Books, 1987.

Bourdieu, Pierre. *Distinction: A Social Critique of the Judgement of Taste.* Cambridge: Mass.: Harvard University Press, 1984.

Braaten, Carl E. *The Future of God.* New York: Harper & Row Publishers, 1969.

Bultmann, Rudolf. *Existence and Faith.* New York: Meridian Books, 1960.

_____. *Jesus Christ and Mythology.* New York: Charles Scribner's Sons, 1951.

_____. *Jesus and the Word.* New York: Charles Scribner's Sons, 1958.

_____. *Theology of the New Testament,* vol. 1. New York: Charles Scribner's Sons, 1951.

Collins, John. *The Apocalyptic Imagination.* New York: Crossroad Books, 1984.

Cone, James H. *For My People: Black Theology and the Black Church.* Maryknoll, N. Y.: Orbis Books, 1984.

_____. *God of the Oppressed.* New York: Seabury Press, 1975.

Cullmann, Oscar. *Christ and Time.* Philadelphia: Westminster Press, 1950.

Davis, Harry R., and Robert C. Good, eds. *Reinhold Niebuhr on Politics.* New York: Charles Scribner's Sons, 1960.

Dillenberger, John, ed. *Martin Luther: Selections from His Writ-*

ings. Garden City, N. Y.: Anchor Books, 1961.

Dodd, C. H. *The Apostolic Preaching and Its Developments*. London: Hodder and Stoughton, 1936.

_____. *Gospel and Law: The Relation of Faith and Ethics in Early Christianity*. New York: Columbia University Press, 1951.

_____. *The Parables of the Kingdom*. New York: Charles Scribner's Sons, 1961.

Finger, Thomas N. *Christian Theology: An Eschatological Approach*, vol. 1. Scottdale, Pa.: Herald Press, 1985.

Foster, Richard J. *Freedom of Simplicity*. San Francisco: Harper & Row Publishers, 1981.

Friesen, Duane K. *Christian Peacemaking and International Conflict*. Scottdale, Pa.: Herald Press, 1986.

_____. "Normative Factors in Troeltsch's Typology of Religious Association." *Journal of Religious Ethics* 3 (Fall 1975): 271-283.

Gabas Pallas, Raul. *Escatologia protestante in la actualidad*. Vitoriensa: Publicationes del Seminario de Vitoria [Spain], vol. 20, 1964.

Garrett, James Leo, ed. *The Concept of the Believers' Church*. Scottdale, Pa.: Herald Press, 1969.

Grant, F. C., ed. *Form Criticism*. New York: Harper & Row Publishers, 1962.

Gustafson, James. *Christ and the Moral Life*. New York: Harper & Row Publishers, 1968.

_____. *Ethics from a Theocentric Perspective*. Chicago: The University of Chicago, vol. 1, 1981; vol. 2, 1984.

_____. "The Sectarian Temptation: Reflections on Theology, the Church, and the

University." *Proceedings of the Catholic Theological Society* 40 (1985): 83- 94.

Hauerwas, Stanley. *Christian Existence Today*. Durham, N. C.: The Labyrinth Press, 1988.

_____. *Suffering Presence*. Notre Dame: University of Notre Dame Press, 1986.

Herzog, Frederick. *Justice Church*. Maryknoll, N. Y.: Orbis Books, 1980.

Jones, L. Gregory. "Should Christians Affirm Rawls' Justice as Fairness? A Response to Professor Beckley." *The Journal of Religious Ethics* 16 (Fall 1988): 251-271.

Kasper, Walter. *Jesus the Christ*. New York: Paulist Press, 1976.

Kass, Leon. *Toward a More Natural Science*. New York: The Free Press, 1985.

Käsemann, Ernst. *New Testament Questions of Today*. Philadelphia: Fortress Press, 1969.

Kovesi, Julius. *Moral Notions*. London: Routledge and Kegan Paul, 1967.

LeMasters, Philip. *The Import of Eschatology in John Howard Yoder's Critique of Constantinianism*. San Francisco: Mellen Research University Press, 1992.

Lohfink, Gerhard. *Jesus and Community*. Philadelphia: Fortress Press, 1984.

MacIntyre, Alasdair. *After Virtue*. Notre Dame: University of Notre Dame Press, 1984.

_____. *Whose Justice? Which Rationality?* Notre Dame: University of Notre Dame Press, 1988.

Marty, Martin, and Dean Peerman, eds. *A Handbook of Christian Theologians*. Nashville: Abingdon Press, 1984.

McCann, Dennis P. *Christian Realism and Liberation Theology*.

Maryknoll, N. Y.: Orbis Books, 1981.

McClendon, James. *Ethics: Systematic Theology,* vol. 1. Nashville: Abingdon Press, 1986.

McNeill, Donald P., Douglas A. Morrison, and Henri J. M. Nouwen. *Compassion: A Reflection on the Christian Life.* Garden City, N. Y.: Doubleday & Company, Inc., 1982.

Metzger, Bruce. *The New Testament: Its Background, Growth, and Content.* Nashville: Abingdon Press, 1983.

Miller, Roman J., and Beryl H. Brubaker, eds. *Bioethics and the Beginning of Life: An Anabaptist Perspective.* Scottdale, Pa.: Herald Press, 1990.

Moltmann, Jürgen. *Theology of Hope: On the Ground and the Implications of a Christian Eschatology.* New York: Harper & Row Publishers, 1967.

Morse, Christopher. *The Logic of Promise in Moltmann's Theology.* Philadelphia: Fortress Press, 1979.

Niebuhr, H. Richard. *Christ and Culture.* New York: Harper & Row Publishers, 1951.

Niebuhr, Reinhold. *An Interpretation of Christian Ethics.* New York: The Seabury Press, 1979. _____. *The Nature and Destiny of Man.* New York: Charles Scribner's Sons, vol. 1, 1941; vol. 2, 1943.

Outka, Gene H., and Paul Ramsey, eds. *Norm and Context in Christian Ethics.* New York: Charles Scribner's Sons, 1968.

Pannenberg, Wolfhart. *Jesus—God and Man.* Philadelphia: The Westminster Press, 1977. _____, ed. *Revelation as History.* New York: The Macmillan Company, 1965.

Pellegrino, Edmund, and David Thomasma, *A Philosophical Basis of Medical Practice.* New York: Oxford University Press, 1981.

Perrin, Norman. *The Kingdom of God in the Teaching of Jesus.* London: SCM Press, 1963.

Pinches, Charles. "Describing Morally: An Inquiry Concerning the Role of Description in Christian Ethics." Ph.D. diss., University of Notre Dame, 1984.

Rabinow, Paul, ed. *The Foucault Reader.* New York: Pantheon Books, 1984.

Ramsey, Paul. *Ethics at the Edges of Life.* New Haven: Yale University Press, 1978. _____. *Fabricated Man: The Ethics of Genetic Control.* New Haven: Yale University Press, 1970. _____. *The Patient as Person.* New Haven: Yale University Press, 1970.

Rawls, John. *A Theory of Justice.* Cambridge: Belknap Press of Harvard University, 1971.

Ritschl, Albrecht. *The Christian Doctrine of Justification and Reconciliation.* Clifton, N. J.: Reference Book Publishers, 1966.

Schweitzer, Albert. *Civilization and Ethics.* London: A & C Black Ltd., 1923. _____. *The Quest for the Historical Jesus.* New York: Macmillan Company, 1968.

Sider, Ronald J. *Rich Christians in an Age of Hunger: A Biblical Study.* Downers Grove, Ill.: InterVarsity Press, 1977. _____, and A. Stephen Barr. "Should the Poor Have Health Care?" *ESA Advocate,* January/February 1990, 1-4.

Simon, Arthur. *Bread for the World.* New York: Paulist Press, 1975.

Sobrino, Jon. *Christology at the Crossroads.* Maryknoll, N. Y.: Orbis Books, 1978.

Tabb, William K., ed. *Churches in Struggle.* New York: Monthly Review Press, 1986.

Troeltsch, Ernst. *The Social Teachings of the Christian Churches.* New York: The MacMillan Company, 1931.

Turner, Bryan. *Religion and Social Theory: A Materialist Perspective.* London: Heinemann Educational Books, 1983.

Wallis, Jim, ed. *Waging Peace: A Handbook for the Struggle to Abolish Nuclear Weapons.* San Francisco: Harper & Row Publishers, 1982.

Walzer, Michael. *Spheres of Justice.* New York: Basic Books, 1983.

Webber, Robert E., and Rodney Clapp. *People of the Truth: The Power of the Worshipping Community in the Modern World.* San Francisco: Harper & Row Publishers, 1988.

Weiss, Johannes. *Jesus' Proclamation of the Kingdom of God.* Philadelphia: Fortress Press, 1971.

Wilder, Amos. *Eschatology and Ethics in the Teaching of Jesus.* New York: Harper & Brothers Publishers, 1939.

Willis, Wendell, ed. *The Kingdom of God in 20th-Century Interpretation.* Peabody: Mass.: Hendrickson Publishers, 1987.

Yoder, John Howard. "Armaments and Eschatology." *Studies in Christian Ethics,* vol. 1, no. 1. Edinburgh: T. & T. Clark Publishers, 1988.

_____. *The Christian Witness to the State.* Newton, Kan.: Faith and Life Press, 1964.

_____. *The Original Revolution.* Scottdale, Pa.: Herald Press, 1971.

_____. *The Politics of Jesus.* Grand Rapids, Mich.: Eerdmans Publishing Company, 1972.

_____. *The Priestly Kingdom.* Notre Dame: University of Notre Dame Press, 1984.

Author Index

A

Arrington, French L., 40, 69, 146, 150
Augustine, 62, 149

B

Barr, A. Stephen, 155
Bartsch, H. W., 144
Beauchamp, Tom, 155
Beker, J. Christiaan, 29, 145
Berkhof, Hendrik, 58-59, 66, 148
Berrigan, Philip, 149
Berryman, Phillip, 147
Bloch, Ernst, 145
Bourdieu, Pierre, 150
Braaten, Carl E., 41, 146
Brubaker, Beryl H., 154
Bultmann, Rudolf, 23-27, 31, 43, 45, 48-50, 135, 137, 141, 144, 147

C

Childress, James, 155
Clapp, Rodney, 65-66, 150
Collins, John, 28-29, 145
Cone, James H., 64, 149
Cullmann, Oscar, 145

D

Davis, Harry R., 151
Dawes, Gil, 147
Dillenberger, John, 153
Dodd, C. H., 22-23, 25, 27, 43, 45, 49-50, 136, 141, 144

F

Finger, Thomas N., 35, 38, 145
Foster, Richard J., 149
Foucault, Michel, 51-54, 58-59, 66, 148

Friesen, Duane K., 92, 100-101, 104-106, 152-153

G

Garrett, James Leo, 154
Good, Robert C., 152
Gustafson, James, 114-126, 128, 136-141, 154-155

H

Hauerwas, Stanley, 131, 148, 155
Hegel, Georg W. F., 145
Heidegger, Martin, 25-26
Herzog, Frederick, 147
Hiers, Richard H., Jr., 23-24, 144, 147

J

Jones, L. Gregory, 99, 101, 152

K

Kant, Immanuel, 82
Kasper, Walter, 37-38, 146
Kass, Leon, 155
Kovesi, Julius, 150
Käsemann, Ernst, 76, 150

L

LeMasters, Philip, 148, 151, 153
Lohfink, Gerhard, 40-41, 127, 146, 155
Luther, Martin, 105-106, 153

M

MacIntyre, Alasdair, 81-82, 85, 98, 100, 151-152, 155
Macquarrie, John, 144
Marty, Martin E., 144
McAlister, Elizabeth, 149

McCann, Dennis P., 93-94, 152
McClendon, James, 61, 149
McNeill, Donald P., 150
Metzger, Bruce M., 146
Miller, Roman J., 154
Moltmann, Jürgen, 33-34, 38, 44-45, 144-146
Morrison, Douglas A., 150

N
Niebuhr, H. Richard, 152
Niebuhr, Reinhold, 91-98, 135, 137-138, 141, 151-152
Nouwen, Henri J. M., 150

P
Pannenberg, Wolfhart, 35-36, 38, 145
Peerman, Dean, 144
Pellegrino, Edmund, 155
Perrin, Norman, 27-29, 145
Pinches, Charles, 151

R
Rabinow, Paul, 148
Ramsey, Paul, 129-130, 155
Rawls, John, 99-100, 152
Rendtorff, Rolf, 30, 145
Ritschl, Albrecht, 20, 143

S
Schweitzer, Albert, 21-22, 27, 31, 43, 45-47, 50, 136, 141, 144, 147
Sider, Ronald J., 149, 155
Simon, Arthur, 147
Sobrino, Jon, 38, 146, 151

T
Tabb, William K., 147
Thomasma, David C., 155
Troeltsch, Ernst, 103-109, 111-114, 121, 124, 126, 128, 137, 139-141, 153
Turner, Bryan, 63, 66, 149-150

W
Wallis, Jim, 149
Walzer, Michael, 100, 152
Webber, Robert E., 65-66, 150
Weiss, Johannes, 20-23, 27, 43, 45, 47-48, 50, 141, 144
Wilder, Amos, 26-27, 43, 45, 48-50, 136-137, 141, 145

Y
Yoder, John Howard, 51-58, 66, 72, 83-84, 86-89, 96-98, 108-114, 126, 138, 148, 151-155

Scripture Index

OLD TESTAMENT

Deuteronomy
15:4 100

Isaiah
32:15 40
35:5-6 127
65:17-25 30

Jeremiah
31:31-34 143

Ezekiel
11:19 40
36:26-27 40
37:1-14 30

Joel
2:28-32 39
3:1-2 40

Amos
9:14 30

NEW TESTAMENT

Matthew 32
6:33 86
10:38 60
11:5 127
11:19 146
11:24-26 61
12:28 22
18:15-18 56
26:64 145
28:19 32
28:20 41

Mark 32
1:14-15 22
1:15 143
1:18 59
8:27-33 146
8:32-33 32

Luke 32
4 90
4:16-21 17
4:18-19 .... 87, 100
4:31-41 87
4:31-44 127
5:12 87
5:12-26 127
5:27-32 87
7:22 127
8:40-56 87
8:43 87
9:1-6 59
9:22-24 87
9:59-62 .... 61, 86
10:9-11 22
11:20 22
12:13-34 87
23:1-5 87
24:21 146
24:26 32

John 32
1:3 .... 46, 80, 90, 116
1:17 32
5:1-18 146
14:26 39
16:28 32

Acts
2 .... 18, 32
2:17 39
2:17-21 154
2:33 143
2:36 .... 32, 145
3:1-10 127

Romans
1:4 .... 32, 40, 46, 154
5:1-2 29
5:2 42
5:8 69
5:12-21 143
6:4 42
6:4-11 .... 61, 86
6:4-14 60
8:18 .... 29, 32
8:23 29
8:29 35
10:4 143
10:9 32
11:17 143
12 .... 59, 71, 90

1 Corinthians 66-77
1:12 67
1:18-31 137
2:6 67
3:1 66-67
3:1-9 67
3:3 66
3:7 66
3:11 66
3:16 66
3:18-19 66

3:18-23 70
4:5 40
4:6-16 67
4:16-17 66-67
4:20 40
5:1—6:8 74
5:1-13 68
5:5 67
5:7-8 67
5:11 70
6 90
6:1-8 68-69
7:1-14 68
7:35 68-69
8:10-11 67-68
9:19 68-69
9:27 67
10:11 18
10:17 60
11:24-26 .... 61, 86
11:26 .... 41, 45, 59, 82
11:27-34 62
12—14 77
12:1—14:40 68
12:1-31 68
12:4-11 67
12:7 71
12:12-31 .... 61, 67
12:22-31 68
12:27 72
13 .... 69, 71
13:1-3 67-68

13:1-13 67-68
13:4-7 67-68
13:8 69
13:9-13 70
13:11 67
14 73
14:1-25 68
14:1-40 .... 68, 70
14:3 57
14:29 57
15:19 33
15:20 35
15:20-24 32
15:20-28 .... 38-39, 143, 145, 154
15:23-28 18
15:24-28 .... 81, 146
15:25 .... 34, 46
15:26-28 41
15:45 40
15:51 38
15:55 130

2 Corinthians
1:20 31
5:17 76

Galatians
1:4 .... 76, 143
3:1-5 40
3:27-28 60
3:27-29 61

5:5 29

Colossians
1:15-16 .... 80, 116
1:15-20 46
3:9-11 61
3:13 65

1 Thessalonians
1:10 29
4:1-8 59
4:14-17 38

Hebrews
8:8-13 143

James
2 .... 71, 90
2:14-26 64

1 Peter
1:5 18

1 John
3 71
4:11 69

Revelation
1:8 .... 46, 80
5:12 83
21:1 .... 33, 143
22:12-13 46

Subject Index

A

Adultery, 91, 150
Advocacy, 133
Alienation, 37, 128
    centrality of, 92
    terms of, 95
Apocalypse, 93
Apocalyptic, 20, 26-31, 33-34, 36-
    38, 43, 135, 146. *See also*
    Eschatology
    Jewish, 21, 24, 28, 30, 34, 38

B

Baptism, 41-42, 59-62, 71, 76, 86, 88
    practices of, 82
Baptist Peace Fellowship of North
    America, 147, 149
Baptized, 60, 62
Believers church, 111-114, 154
Bioethical issues, 154
Bioethics, 154
Blacks, 64
Bread for the World, 147, 149

C

Casuistry, 96, 98
Catholic Worker movement, 149
Charlemagne, 110
Christ. *See also* Jesus, Christ
Christocentric, 45
Christology, 38, 116. *See also* Jesus,
    Christology
Chronically ill, 131
Church, 18-19, 31, 39-42, 45, 47-48,
    50-52, 54-55, 58-62, 65-67,
    69-77, 79, 84, 88, 91, 99, 103-
    105, 107, 109-110, 112-116,
    121, 123-125, 127-128, 131-

132, 138-140, 146-147. *See*
    also Ecclesiology;
    Eschatology
church-sect distinction, 104-106
communal formation, 107, 118,
    132-133, 138
community, 18, 40, 42, 91, 126,
    128, 139-140
community of discipleship, 18,
    141
community of faith, 42, 52-53,
    55, 66, 70, 75, 86, 89-91, 98,
    103, 107-108, 117-118, 127,
    138-140, 150
community of presence, 65
distinct community, 58
eschatological, 48
eschatological community, 18,
    40, 53, 65, 139, 147
faithfulness of, 115
practice, 59, 62, 64, 149
practices of, 31, 42, 58-59, 61-62,
    72-74, 77, 81-82, 86, 107
social production of, 17, 51, 58,
    77
type, 104-106
Community, 124, 128
    alternative, 126
Compassion, 150
Compromise, 107-110, 114
    ethic of, 109
Constantine (the Great), 108
"Constantinian(ism)," 108-110, 114,
    124-125, 133, 148, 151, 153
Corinth, 66. *See also* 1 Cor. in
    Scripture Index
Creation, 36, 46, 59, 76, 80-82, 89,
    95, 108, 112, 116, 118, 122-
    123, 126, 128, 140-141

165

Creator, 117
Cross, 34-35, 65, 86, 96-97, 113, 137

D

Death, 19, 37, 60-61, 128, 130-132, 137
Demons, 22
Demythologize, 25
Desires, 64
Disciple(s), 19, 21, 32, 46, 54, 56, 58-59, 61, 72, 82, 84, 86, 89-90, 94, 111, 116, 118-120, 126, 128-132, 141
Discipleship, 17, 50, 52, 55, 57-58, 60, 64, 70-73, 76-77, 79-82, 84, 86-87, 89-91, 93-101, 103, 107-110, 112-114, 116-118, 120, 122-128, 131-133, 135, 139-141. *See also* Ethics; Practical
  characteristics of, 108
  community of, 18, 45, 49, 59, 62, 123, 138, 140
  ethic of, 124-125
  formation, 128
  medical, 132
  practice of, 70, 77, 85, 101, 117, 138-139
  requirements of, 139
  social production of, 70
Disciplines, 128
Dispositions, 67-70, 72-73. *See also* Love; Virtues

E

Ecclesiology, 18, 42, 45, 72-73, 106, 113, 123, 140. *See also* Church
Economics, 75, 87, 115, 117
Education, 63
Empathy, 129
Employment, 63
Enlightenment, 44
Environmental destruction, 75
Eschatology, 19, 26-27, 30-31, 33, 36, 38-39, 41-43, 45-52, 54, 56, 66, 69-70, 73, 75-76, 79-80, 82-85, 88-89, 92-94, 97-98, 103, 105-108, 110, 113-116, 118, 121-129, 133, 135, 137, 140-141, 146, 151. *See*
  also Apocalyptic; Church; Future; Hope
  Christian, 18, 20, 30-31, 33, 38, 48
  Eschaton, 18, 59-60, 62, 116, 118, 126, 128, 135, 137
  futuristic, 18, 22, 47
  Jewish, 27-31
  realized, 22-23
  recent views of, 20
  scheme, 108
  thoroughgoing, 21
Ethics, 20-21, 26-27, 42-43, 45-49, 52, 54, 56, 61, 72, 80, 109, 115, 119, 122. *See also* Discipleship; Practical; Sin
  Christian, 17-20, 23, 25-26, 41-42, 44, 49-50, 53-55, 70, 73, 77, 80, 94-95, 97, 103-104, 106-107, 112, 114-115, 120-121, 124, 138-139, 141
  communitarian, 118, 123, 133
  decision making, 56
  discipleship, 124-125, 133, 139, 141, 153
  interim, 21, 26
  medical, 126-127, 129-130, 133, 140, 155
  practice of, 99
  sexual immorality, 59, 66, 68, 74
  social, 52
  theological, 19, 27
  withdrawal, 116
Evangelicals for Social Action, 147, 149, 155
Evil, 35, 39, 47, 87, 130. *See also* Sin
Existentialism, 24-26, 48
Expectation. *See* Apocalyptic; Eschatology; Hope

F

Future, 18, 29-31, 33-34, 36, 38, 41, 47-49, 61, 65, 67, 76-77, 83-84, 86, 94-95, 111, 122-123, 135-136, 139-140, 143. *See also* Eschatology

G

Genetic engineers, 129
God. *See* Creation; Creator; Providence; Trinity

Gospel, 32, 43
Government, 63, 117
Grace, 64, 70, 112

H
Habits, 62, 64
Habituation, 59, 64
Healing, 59, 87, 127, 129
Health care insurance, 155
Historicist, 136
"History-making" event, 136
Holy Spirit. *See* Spirit, Holy
Hope, 30, 32-34, 36, 51, 67-71, 73-
    74, 76-77, 82-83, 93, 95, 97,
    122-123, 130, 135, 137, 139,
    143, 146, 150. *See also*
    Eschatology
  Christian, 18, 38-39, 42
  Jewish, 37
Human rights, 100
Hunger, 149

I
In vitro fertilization, 155
Israel, 35, 137. *See also* Eschatology,
    Jewish

J
Jesus, 17, 20-22, 32, 35-36, 40, 43,
    46-49, 59, 61, 71-73, 77, 80,
    86, 95, 97, 100, 103, 107, 110,
    114-116, 119-121, 124, 140.
    See also Cross
  as preacher, 43
  ascension of, 39
  Christ, 32, 36-37, 40, 45-46, 53,
    66, 70, 89, 112, 118, 123
  Christocentric, 37-39
  Christological, 123
  Christology, 31, 33
  description of, 44
  exaltation of, 37
  healing, 127
  Messiah, 31-32, 38-39, 41, 49, 84,
    119
  ministry of, 26, 43, 45, 49, 61, 75
  moral relevance of, 136
  moral teacher, 43
  nonresistant, 96
  nonviolence, 96
  of Nazareth, 30, 38-39, 52, 70, 89

parables of, 22
preaching of, 20-23, 25-28, 43,
    135
resurrection of, 17-19, 28-29, 31-
    51, 53, 55, 59, 61, 63, 66, 69,
    73, 75, 77, 79, 81-82, 84, 86,
    88, 93-95, 97-98, 107, 111,
    114, 121-124, 126, 129-130,
    135-137, 140-141, 143, 146-
    147
risen Lord, 19, 31-35, 37-43, 45-
    47, 49, 51, 54, 59, 61, 76-77,
    80-81, 83-84, 86-89, 94-95,
    97-98, 100-101, 107-108,
    110, 114, 117, 122-126, 128,
    132, 135-140
teachings of, 49
John the Baptist, 21
Jonah House, 149
Jurisprudence, 154
Just-war tradition, 86-87, 96
Justice, 38-39, 65, 74, 79-80, 85, 89-
    101, 106, 133, 139, 150-151
  conception of, 101
  description of, 92
  of God, 39
  practice of, 99
  views of, 99, 101
  virtue of, 99

K
Kingdom, 17-23, 25-29, 31-50, 54-
    55, 59-62, 65-66, 69, 71, 73-
    77, 82, 84, 86-87, 92-98, 100-
    101, 105-110, 113-114, 120-
    128, 130-131, 133, 135-138,
    140-141, 143

L
Liberalism, Protestant, 20
Lord's Supper, 41-42, 45, 59-62, 71,
    82, 86, 88, 149
Love, 37, 55, 65, 67-71, 74, 91-92,
    94-96, 98, 150. *See also*
    Dispositions; Virtues
  law of, 92

M
Marriage, 91
Media, 64
Medical. *See also* Ethics, medical;
    Healing; Health

indications policy, 130
palliative care, 130
practice, 115, 128, 132, 154-155
Mennonite Central Committee, 149
Messiah, 87, 110, 119, 121, 137. *See
    also* Jesus, Messiah
    of Israel, 38
Moral
    description, 19, 79-81, 90-91, 94-
        95, 101, 103
    development, 149
    discernment, 79, 108, 119, 139
    formation, 58-60, 63, 67, 74, 117-
        118, 125, 131, 138, 149
    philosophy, 19
    rationality, 19, 85, 90, 97-98, 101
    reasoning, 57, 83
Mysticism, 104, 106

N
Narrative, 28, 61, 80-82, 84-86, 88,
    90, 93-95, 97-98, 107-108,
    110, 115, 122, 127, 130, 139,
    151
Natural sciences, 117-118, 121-122,
    125, 136, 154
Needy, the, 101
New Testament scholarship, 19
New age, 17-19, 29, 35, 38-43, 45-
    51, 53-54, 59, 63, 66, 69-70,
    73-75, 77, 79, 82, 86, 89-90,
    93-95, 98, 101, 114, 121-129,
    135-137, 140-141, 143, 147-
    148
Nicene Creed, 33
Nonviolence, 96-98
Nuclear
    holocaust, 83
    war, 75
    weapons, 149

O
Oppression, 100

P
Pacifism, 97
Parousia, 18, 29, 41-42, 47, 50-51,
    59, 62, 69-70, 72-73, 82-84,
    94, 97, 107, 130, 135-137,
    143, 147. *See also*
    Eschatology

Patriotism, 75
Paul, 21, 29, 31-32, 35, 40, 59, 62,
    65-70, 73-74, 76-77, 90, 143
    theology of, 29
Pentecost, 18, 39, 41-43, 46-47, 50-
    51, 59, 62, 69-70, 75, 82-84,
    94, 97, 107, 130, 135-139,
    143, 146-147
Peter, 32
Philosophy, 117
Physical healing. *See* Healing; Jesus,
    healing; Medical
Politics, 115
Poor, the, 87, 90, 101, 132, 155
Poverty, 100
Power, 40, 52, 55, 65, 98, 123, 128
    abuse of, 94
    balance of, 92-96, 98
    distribution of, 94
    structures of, 63
Powers, the, 58, 60, 73, 77, 119, 121,
    124-125
Practical. *See also* Discipleship;
    Ethics
    discernment, 67
    rationality, 79, 85, 87, 91, 101,
        117
    rationality, Christian, 85, 89
    rationality, Humean, 85
    reason, 19, 53, 56-57, 73, 79, 85-
        89, 94-95, 98, 100, 103, 108,
        110, 117, 155
    reason, discipleship, 140-141
    reasoning, Aristotelian, 85
    reasoning, Thomistic, 85
    wisdom, 57
Providence, 109-110, 113-114, 120,
    124-126

R
Racism, 64, 75
Realism, Christian, 93
Redemption, 37, 46, 80-82, 84-85,
    91, 93, 95, 97, 101, 107-108,
    122-124, 128, 133, 140-141
Repentance, 26
Resistance, 58-59, 63, 77, 128
Resurrection, 31-36, 42, 44, 61, 97,
    121, 137, 140. *See also* Jesus,
    resurrection of
    history-making event, 45

Righteousness, 26

S
Salvation, 19, 26, 28, 32, 41, 46-47,
    49, 55, 60, 64, 67, 73, 76-77,
    89, 93-95, 98, 127, 139
Science(s), 119-125, 137, 140
Scripture, 57. *See also* Scripture
    Index
Sect(s), Sectarian, 19, 103-104, 109-
    111, 113-115, 133, 139-141,
    153-154
Sin, 19, 34-35, 37, 55, 60, 62, 64, 75-
    76, 92, 95, 97, 108, 111, 128,
    137. *See also* Ethics; Evil
Slavery, 100
Social Gospel, 20
Social inequality, 75
Social sciences, 19, 117, 154
Society of Biblical Literature, 28-29
Spirit, Holy, 18-19, 39-42, 45-47, 49,
    51, 57-59, 65-67, 69, 71-72,
    75-76, 84-85, 89, 94, 110,
    112, 117, 121, 123-124, 127-
    128, 138-139, 143, 146-147
Spiritualist, 111-113
Suffering, 131
Synoptics, 22. *See also* Scripture
    Index

T
Tastes, 64
Theocentric piety, 120, 124
Theocrats, 111-113
Theology. *See also* specific topics
    Christian, 18, 26
    Old Testament, 30
    of Paul, 29. *See also* Paul
    systematic, 19
Theoreticism, 53
Torah, 34
Trinity, 46

U
United States of America, 93

V
Violence, 96-98
Virtues, 68-72, 99, 138. *See also*
    Dispositions; Love
    patience, 129

W
War, 86
Wealth, 75, 90
Women, equality of, 75

The Author

Philip LeMasters was born in 1964 and raised in Beaumont, Texas. He graduated in 1984 from the University Scholars Program at Baylor University in Waco, Texas, where he focused his studies on religion and Greek. During 1985-87, he was a graduate student in religious studies at Rice University in Houston, Texas, earning an M.A. degree in ethics. Then he enrolled in the Graduate Program in Religion at Duke University in Durham, North Carolina, from which he received the Ph.D. degree in Christian theology and ethics in 1990. His doctoral dissertation, *The Import of Eschatology in John Howard Yoder's Critique of Constantinianism*, was published in 1992 by Mellen Research University Press.

LeMasters was visiting assistant professor of religion at Wake Forest University, Winston-Salem, North Carolina, where he taught courses in Christian ethics during 1991-92. He taught Christian ethics and Old Testament in the Department of Religious Studies and Philosophy at Gardner-Webb College in Boiling Springs, North Carolina, in the spring term of 1991. During 1989-90 he served as a teaching assistant in both Christian theology and Christian ethics at Duke Divinity School. From 1985 to 1987 he assisted in courses in both comparative religions and ethics at Rice University and taught Christian education classes for adults in a number of congregations in Houston and Beaumont. He is a member of Phi Beta Kappa, the American Academy of Religion, the National Association of Baptist Professors of Religion, the Society of Christian Ethics, the Baptist Peace Fellowship of North America, Evangelicals for Social Action, Bread for the World, and Amnesty International.

LeMasters has published essays or reviews in *The Christian Century, Theology Today, Encounter, Perspectives in Religious Studies, Auslegung,* and *Church Divinity,* a Monograph Series of the Graduate Theological Foundation. He has also presented a number of scholarly papers at regional and national meetings of the American Academy of Religion.

LeMasters is married to Paige Humes LeMasters, M.D. They reside in Thomasville, North Carolina, and are members of Emerywood Baptist Church in nearby High Point, North Carolina.